THE
11th
HABIT

THE
11th
HABIT

Design Your Company Culture to Foster the Habits of High Performance

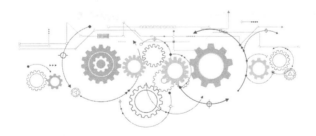

ANDREW SYKES
AND HANLIE VAN WYK

HABITS AT WORK
CHICAGO, IL

Published by
Habits At Work
Chicago, IL
habitsatwork.com

Publisher's Cataloging-in-Publication Data
Sykes, Andrew.

The 11th habit : design your company culture to foster the habits of high performance / Andrew Sykes and Hanlie van Wyk. – Chicago, IL : Habits At Work, 2019.

p. ; cm.

ISBN13: 978-0-9980235-0-2

1. Corporate culture. 2. Organizational behavior. 3. Organizational effectiveness. I. Title. II. van Wyk, Hanlie.

HD58.7.S95 2019
302.35—dc23   2018956552

Interior design by Brooke Camfield

Printed in the United States of America
23   22   21   20   19   •   5   4   3   2   1

Contents

Acknowledgments   vii

In memoriam: Jim Rivett   xi

Introduction   xiii

1 Building a High-Performance Company   1

2 Habits Create Your Destiny   25

3 Habits That Matter   39

4 The World of Context   71

5 The Four Powers   87

6 The Context of the Self:
   Managing our Mind-Sets   113

7 The Social Context:
   Harnessing the Power of Social Contagion   133

8 The Spaces Context:
   Build for Good Habits   153

9 The Systems Context:
   Make Processes Work for You   181

10 Putting It All Together   213

About the Authors   221

Acknowledgments

Shakespeare said, "It's not in the stars to hold our destiny, but in ourselves." If that's true in my case, it's only because of the fortunate choices I've made in the people in my life. This book would never have started were it not for the persistent nudging of Lynn Rust Henderson—a dear friend whose persistence has paid off. Book one is finally complete! Caryn Tomasiewicz, my cofounder at Habits at Work, was my other great inspiration for writing this book. We worked together, learned together, and have tackled writing projects together, in this case at the same time but different books. Whatever Habits at Work becomes in the future, Caryn's influence will always be remembered, and the same is true for my life.

It would never have gotten finished if not for the hundreds of hours of fact-checking, researching, rewriting, editing, hand-wringing, and gentle pestering of my dear friends and work colleagues Hanlie Van Wyk and Colin Bullen. Hanlie is responsible for the parts of this book that are well researched and well written, Colin for the parts that are logical, witty, or insightful. I'm afraid I'm to blame for the balance. Hanlie spent more time fixing what I wrote than I spent writing, and so this book is at least as much hers as it is mine. She leads BRATLAB and has been a personal friend and anchor in my life for more than 20 years.

Like most things at Habits at Work, this book was in many ways a team effort. Tia Pappas, Gloria Gong, and Bree Miller were not directly involved in writing this book but did do many hours of research that found its way into the book, provided weeks of debate with me about topics in the book, or provided encouragement and kept the lights on while I took my sweet time completing many drafts. In that way, their thoughts and ideas are found in the pages of this book. Thank you to each and every one of you from the bottom of my heart. This book, and our company, Habits at Work, would not be the same without your presence, your passion, and your support. It all will never be forgotten.

After getting halfway through this book, I discovered that professional help was in order. We found and hired Malcolm Nicholl to help us cull the book from several hundred pages to its more digestible final form, to correct my poor writing and grammar, and to add the touch of a professional writer. I am grateful for your patience and your clear ideas on making this book more readable.

I've discovered, as have many authors, that writing a book has a price: hours away from family members and the bad moods that at least this author often came home with after a few frustrating hours of writing. For putting up with me, during the writing of this book and at all other times, I am so grateful to my wonderful wife, Maddie. Of course, that's the least that you do for me. This book is written in your honor, as my own small token of love and appreciation for the wonderful person you are, the lessons in how to live life that you have taught me, and your love and patience with what can only be described as your "high-maintenance husband."

Last and certainly not least, my inspiration for writing this book: my three beautiful children, Lexington, Islay, and Caroline. My greatest dream is that you will one day work at a company that takes the ideas in this book and brings them to life. You deserve this and so much more. I have had the pleasure of living and working on six continents and visiting many countries. I've had grand adventures and seen much of what the world has to offer. Yet that all pales in comparison to the joy I feel when I watch each of you learn, grow, and become the kinds of human beings that I'm still struggling to become as my half century of life approaches. I will always have the habit of being the proudest dad on the planet. I love you all endlessly.

In memoriam: Jim Rivett

Jim was more than just a client. He inspired me, personally, in my life and my work. His story was one of the main catalysts that inspired this book. Overflowing with empathy and kindness, passionate, quirky, interesting, interested and just a whole lot of fun . . . Jim, you will be dearly missed by this world.

Introduction

[hab-it]
**an acquired behavior pattern regularly followed
until it has become almost involuntary**

We acquire an abundance of habits during our lifetime—some good, some bad. Creating good habits and getting rid of bad ones can powerfully transform personal lives and business entities. It can help individuals get exactly what they want in life: to be healthy, happy, and secure. And good habits can help companies achieve a difficult-to-copy competitive advantage.

Employee habits create your company's destiny. Your future success depends on your ability to change your habits and those of your employees. But what kind of habits matter most? How and when do you infuse them into the lifeblood of your organization? What difference can you expect them to make? Since many people spend a third of their total waking hours at work, the most logical place to make changes is at the workplace itself—and not only for the future of the organization but also for each individual's personal future.

Over the past decade, we have researched why people find it hard to create positive, life-enriching habits and, more importantly, exactly how to go about making such habits a natural part of their lives. The outcome of our research is our Four Powers model that plays out in four life contexts that anyone can design to generate the right kind of habits. The four life contexts are the conditions that surround us, within which we live our lives:

1. The Context of the SELF—Our personal thoughts, emotions, decisions, self-narratives, beliefs, values, and filters imposed on information coming in from the outside world.
2. The SOCIAL Context—Our interactions with other people, including family, friends, coworkers, and peer groups.
3. The SPACES Context—The environments in which we live, work, and play, such as our homes, offices, schools, public places, and, more recently, virtual spaces.
4. The SYSTEMS Context—The rules, policies, laws, cultural norms, incentives, traditions, and routines that surround and permeate our lives.

The Four Powers actively stimulate new habits are the powers to:

1. Grow CAPABILITY—Developing the competence and confidence to succeed.
2. Inspire MOTIVATION—Compelling us into action to create new habits.
3. Overcome BARRIERS—Getting around, breaking through, or leaping over the obstacles that get in the way.
4. Resist TEMPTATION—Avoiding and/or fighting off the everyday distractions that keep us from practicing good habits.

When you grow capability and inspire motivation, you can overcome barriers and resist temptation. This is the dynamic framework that's the product of 10 years of discovery at our Behavioral Research and Applied Technology Laboratory (BRATLAB) and our two decades of business development experience on six continents, working with some of the world's largest companies including Google, Shell Oil Company, McDonald's, Nokia, BAE Systems, Unilever, Blue Cross Blue Shield, and many others.

Within the BRATLAB framework we have put together a collection of research that explains:

- The habits that are worth pursuing and to what extent for maximum benefit.
- The return on investment a company can expect when its people adopt these habits.
- How to scale habit design across your company as a way to future-proof your business, by fostering high-performance teams. (Future-proofing is a means of protecting your organization, product, or any system from becoming obsolete.)

Our team of actuaries, researchers, and behavioral consultants has structured solutions specifically designed to help employers:

- Assess their organizations' capacity for creating new employee habits.
- Identify the greatest opportunities for rapid improvement.
- Design a vision and a vision scorecard for employee performance and a matching strategy to bring them to life.
- Plan and execute a clear road map to implement these strategies.
- Figure out how to make it easy and natural for employees to ensure that they practice what we call "pivotal habits," the habits that create health, happiness, and financial security.
- How to choose "habit prescriptions" that will help you design your destiny as an organization.

What does it mean for the forward-thinking CEO, senior executives, and company owners? When performed effectively, results typically include:

- Lower overhead such as health-related expenses and recruitment, training and retraining costs.
- Higher levels of employee engagement and personal and job-related productivity.
- Improved overall company performance.

Employees who look after themselves are employees with the capacity to become high-performance employees. And they can help you create a high-performance company.

At BRATLAB we spend a lot of time and effort sifting through and differentiating between high-quality, reliable, and trustworthy research and the numerous marketing white papers, case studies, and other "wishful thinking" articles (even those that appear in reputable journals) that are not so dependable. Our research has shown that people want to be healthy, happy, and secure, but all too often they lay the blame for being unfit, stressed, and financially hobbled at the door of their company. They work physically and mentally injurious hours because it's the company culture and it's expected of them.

You may be wondering why we called this book *The 11th Habit*.

Here's why:

> *We believe that there are 10 common habits that make all, or most, employees great at their particular job. I'll provide more details on those habits in the final chapter. However, there is an 11th Habit—the habit of self-care—that is not directly part of our jobs but that prepares each one of us to be our best selves and, as a result, to be great at our jobs. But there is a second reason: the habit of self-care, or, rather, the set of habits*

that make up looking after ourselves, is something we all tend to ignore until it's too late. We leave things to the eleventh hour! In this book, we recognize that as employees, we're just as guilty as our employers in prioritizing the needs of customers and shareholders over our own needs and our own health, happiness, and security in particular. We've written this book to make the case to CEOs that they should design their companies with employee well-being as the first habit and not leave it until it's too late or until employees "fall over," cost us money, or are absent from their jobs or ready to quit from burnout. So, while the habit of self-care might be the one we finally get to, it really should be the habit that we start with, and that's what this book is all about.

Another reason for writing this book was to bridge the gap between the best academic research and the contrasting opinions held by most business leaders. As we will see, a compelling case can be made for the role of improved health, happiness, and security to improve company performance. Our "formula" for creating positive habits is based on not only a wealth of academic research but also a thorough analysis of practical applications successfully deployed in a range of industries. It is a road map that senior executives can follow to help their company thrive.

In an ever-changing working world, good employee habits are a rock-solid underpinning for long-term success. Our mission is to help companies flourish through the success of their people rather than at the expense of their people. We aid companies in becoming "high-performance" employers that keep pace with the emerging skills needed to stay ahead of the game. In this book, I share the essence of what I have learned and what I now present at seminars and workshops for company owners, CEOs, and other corporate executives.

If you're a senior executive who really means it when you say that "people are our most important asset" and wants to act in a way that's authentic and true to that statement, this book is for you. If you're a business leader who is prepared to think deeply about human nature, competitive advantage, human performance, and the best ways to build a robust and dynamically successful business, read on. You might have to stop, think, and chew on some of the ideas. In fact, we hope *The 11th Habit* provides you with a lot more than food for thought and compels you to take action, because vision without execution counts for nothing.

1

Building a High-Performance Company

We are what we repeatedly do.
Excellence, then, is not an act but a habit.

—Will Durant in *The Story of Philosophy:*
The Lives and Opinions of the
World's Greatest Philosophers

How do you judge a company as a high-performance organization? What sets it apart from the competition? What do you have to do to climb to those dizzy heights and stay at the top? Harvard Business School professor and best-selling author Michael Porter suggests that the benchmark should be "higher than industry average return on capital employed" (ROCE). His point: if you're not able to return more per dollar invested in your company than similar businesses, you're wasting shareholders' money, and they would be better off investing in competing businesses (or in an industry index fund).

In our view, high ROCE, on its own, doesn't fully capture the concept of a high-performing company. We therefore add *high growth* to the definition, where "high" is defined as greater than industry average. Growth in new markets, in new products, or even simply in new revenue is necessary for long-term sustainability of any business.

> **DEFINITION:** A high-performance company is one that generates both higher than industry average return on capital employed and high growth.

Expert opinions on the ways to become a high-performance company are numerous and varied.

Jim Collins wrote several of the more famous books on the topic, including *Good to Great, Built to Last, Great by Choice,* and, more recently, *How the Mighty Fall,* in which he outlines many logical concepts to explain high performance, from "getting the right people on the bus" (First Who, then What) to the "Hedgehog concept" concentrating on the intersection of (1) what you are deeply passionate about, (2) what you can be the best in the world at, and (3) what best drives your economic or resource engine. Other concepts include the importance of market timing, the power of networking, the relevance of storytelling excellence, building a sales-driven culture, and the impact of marketing and promotions.

Which of these drivers of business success are essential? The simple answer is **all of them**. But to get to the bottom line, you have to ask, **What do all of the drivers of corporate high performance and competitive advantage have *in common*?**

Although leadership is considered to be a personality trait or a "gift," it is the *acts* of great leaders that really make them successful.

It is the repetitive telling of stories outlining the future, in a way that inspires people to join them to create that future. The suggestion that leaders paint an exciting vision and then exit stage left, leaving it to the managers to build that future, is a myth. Leadership requires constant repetition and constant attention to the details. Complaints of micro-managing had been leveled against Steve Jobs and other renowned leaders. We don't see it that way. They all spent a lot of time on the details, making sure that every single employee understood not only the overall vision but also their specific role in achieving that vision.

Similarly, being an effective manager requires giving people frequent constructive feedback that motivates them to try harder, take new risks, and assume responsibility for the outcomes. It is a fine line between watching over people's shoulder and giving them the space and autonomy to deliver their best work on their own. Execution involves the coordinated effort of the workforce—sometimes hundreds of thousands of people—fulfilling their roles and tasks with high fidelity. Look at most people's role, especially as positions become ever-more specialized, and you'll find that the most important aspect revolves around just a few actions done well, time and time again.

In essence, what all these drivers of performance have in common is that they are made up by or created by the habits of employees, managers, and leaders. Business leaders are increasingly cognizant that their role must include designing and owning the culture of their organization. Culture gives them the leverage to attract the best talent, to support innovation and agility, and to ensure the highest levels of performance. But what do we mean by "culture," and how is it related to employee habits?

What's a Culture of Performance?

Corporate culture is often considered to be somewhat mysterious, or at least difficult to define, measure, or design. The apparent mystery can be solved when we view culture through the lens of habits. Culture, in effect, is the sum of the behaviors of the people in a company: what they say, what they do, and how they do it. It may be influenced by the way people think, the stories they tell, the way leadership behaves, the values employees and managers hold dear, and the way the organization is designed. But culture itself is just the sum of all the things done and not done and repeated over time. The fact that culture derives from the collection of employee habits makes it a somewhat stable phenomenon, while also being one of the reasons why changing cultures seems to be so difficult. Good and bad habits can be hard to break!

DEFINITION: Culture is the sum of the habits of all employees. It is "the way we do things around here."

Leaders who wish to design a culture of performance are therefore in the business of designing performance habits for their employees.

But What Do Employees Really Want?

At BRATLAB, we first examined the question "What do employees really want?" in the belief that if employers could ensure the life success of each employee, they would gain not only loyalty but also exceptional performance. However, the common retort from employees was, "What makes you think my boss has any idea what I think success looks like for my own life?" In response, we developed the "Everyperson Test" to ask that question of employees. In essence, we said, "You're right, so you tell us."

The Everyperson Test

Take a few moments to reflect on the following questions and write down your answers. By doing so you will find greater value from the balance of this chapter, since you will have your own answers as a reference point.

- What does success mean for me in my own life?
- What do I really want for myself and for my life?
- Why do I want these things in my life? (This question can deepen the answers you provide.)

We include the Everyperson Test in most of our keynote talks, training programs, and workshops, so we've posed these questions to thousands of people. Occasionally, we get some curious and unconventional answers. About one in 100 people say they want to be famous, or live to 150, or travel to another planet, or something just as outlandish. However, the vast majority give answers that fall into three categories.

Categorizing Answers to the Everyperson Test

Most people's answers fall into one of three categories—Health, Happiness, and Security.

Health: People want to be healthy or reap the rewards from being healthy, such as living longer, being active, pursuing hobbies, spending time outdoors, and playing with their kids or grandchildren.

Happiness: People want to be happy. Many say exactly that and simply want joy in their lives. However, happiness is a much richer concept and includes making a difference in the lives of others, forging meaningful and fulfilling relationships, and having autonomy in and mastery over one's work.

Security: People want to be secure, by which they generally mean financially secure. They may express this as wanting to be rich or well paid, or having a lot of money in the bank, or having the things that money can buy (a nice house, cars, luxury goods, or experiences). Most answers boil down to wanting to live a good life, free of financial stress, and not scraping to make ends meet each month. Answers include being able to cover emergencies, retire comfortably, and take care of one's kids and grandkids. For some people, security is as basic as personal safety (in their homes or in their neighborhoods). In today's high-tech world, security includes data privacy, especially the protection of one's identity and personal assets.

Sadly, although everyone seems to answer the Everyperson Test with the same three desires, these are aspirations that most Americans don't achieve.

Are Employees Healthy?

Let's look at health. While 60 percent of Americans say they are in average or good health, a recent Oregon State University study estimated that only 2.7 percent of the US adult population consistently practices four key healthy lifestyle habits: regular exercise, not smoking, maintaining a healthy weight, and eating a healthy diet. A few other statistics paint a grim picture of our health:

- Almost 70 percent of American adults are overweight or obese (NIDDK).
- Life expectancy at birth for Americans is 81.6 years for women and 76.9 years for men (an average of 79.3 years, according to the WHO) and ranks thirty-first (WHO), forty-third (UN), or fiftieth (CIA) out of a list of advanced countries, behind China (Hong Kong) and Japan, which

lead the pack at 83–84 years—this despite the fact that the United States has the highest GPD per capita.

- Worse, the United States appears to be the only first-world country that suffers from deteriorating middle-aged mortality rates, especially among white males. Diabetes, liver cancer (very much caused by alcohol abuse), suicide (linked to increasing depression), and drug overdoses explain most of that increase. Opioid and other prescription-drug-related deaths are a particular concern that is finally getting some attention.

- One in three adults suffers from raised blood pressure or hypertension (CDC).

- Eighty percent of adults do not meet the guidelines for aerobic and muscle-strengthening activities, and less than 5 percent participate in 30 minutes of physical activity every day.

- Twenty-four percent of adults say they suffer from **extreme** stress that manifests in physical symptoms, while an increasing percentage of adults report experiencing at least one symptom of stress with every passing year.

It is not just our actual health that is poor. Our perception of our own health is far from accurate. The greater the extent of a person's obesity, for instance, the less accurate his or her perception of the excess weight. This misperception determines and negatively impacts the lifestyle choices a person makes when addressing his or her health habits.

We are winning the war on some diseases such as lung cancer, because of either medical advances or changes in lifestyle, such as quitting the smoking habit. However, for our biggest health challenges, including cancer and heart disease, the dominant driver remains poor habits that medical advances can't cure. When people do admit to shortcomings in their health habits, the list of reasons is revealing. They say things like:

- "I don't have enough time to work out."
- "When I come home from work, I'm too tired to exercise."
- "Healthy food is not available at work," or "takes too long to prepare," or "is expensive," or "doesn't taste as good as McDonald's."
- "We're expected to be always on, and I've not slept well in years."
- "I check email right up to the minute I go to bed and the minute I wake up. I never get to switch off."

Sound familiar? Note that most people's excuses directly point to work as the cause of their inability to practice a healthy lifestyle. Work is an easy target and, to a large extent, a justified one, because, one way or another, we spend so much of our lives working. If we're looking for a scene of the crime, the workplace is a better candidate than our own homes.

When we talk to people about the main drivers of their health, they often point to outliers that seem to refute the statistics. We hear them reference their great uncle Joe, who, despite smoking 40 cigarettes a day, lived to be 103 or, at the other end of the spectrum, vibrant young adults who pursued an extremely healthy lifestyle but were struck down by a heart attack. Let's not forget: these are *outliers* and not representative of the population as a whole. It's incontrovertible that there is a very strong causal relationship between our lifestyles—our health habits—and the health we enjoy.

Are Employees Happy?

The United States is rightly proud of the declaration of rights, promising every citizen the right to life, liberty, and the pursuit of happiness. No guarantees are given about the attainment of that happiness, or there might be a long line of people asking for their money back. In the realm of happiness, there is a similar disconnect between what people say and what the statistics demonstrate. When asked, only 33 percent of American adults say they are "happy with their lives." And consider these numbers:

- America ranks number one globally in income per capita yet only thirteenth in happiness levels.
- More than one in 10 Americans regularly takes an antidepressant. Between 1988 and 2008, the rate of antidepressant use increased nearly 400 percent.
- Seventy-four percent of American workers cite their level of work stress as significant, causing half of them to contemplate quitting. Stress alone costs US companies more than $300 billion a year.

As with health, our habits play a large role in determining our level of happiness. Although about 40 percent of our overall happiness is estimated to be so-called set-point happiness, over which we may have little control, the balance is determined by the lives we choose to lead and specifically the habits we practice. How we invest in relationships, what we do with our time, how we relate to our jobs, and many other choices we make leave us feeling either content, inspired, and fulfilled or stressed, depressed, and unhappy.

Despite our apparent right to the pursuit of happiness, for many it remains elusive. After nearly 250 years as a nation, Americans should expect to be better at understanding not only how to pursue happiness but also how to attain it! And a special note: according to a landmark study by a team of researchers at the prestigious London School of Economics, happiness is derived much more from health and friends than it is from wealth. The study, called "Origins of

Happiness," analyzed data from four countries including the United States and found that, on average, people have not become any happier over the past 50 years, even though average incomes have more than doubled. In recommending that governments make measuring people's satisfaction with their lives a priority, they found that eliminating depression and anxiety would reduce unhappiness by 20 percent compared to just 5 percent from the elimination of poverty. Lord Richard Layard, who led the research, said, "Tackling depression and anxiety would be four times as effective as tackling poverty. It would also pay for itself."

Are Employees Secure?

What about financial security? As a nation we're not optimally healthy or happy, but perhaps we're secure? After all, Americans enjoy the highest average income per capita on the planet, the third-highest average GDP per capita, and one of the lowest rates of poverty. For many people around the world, the United States still remains the dream country where you have the best chance to improve your standard of living. Scratch below the surface, however, and you find a less rosy picture. More than 90 percent of the wealth is in the hands of just 10 percent of the population. American's median wealth (rather than the average) comes nineteenth in world rankings. The super-rich obscure the fact that the average person is struggling:

- Forty percent of people say they find it difficult to meet monthly expenses.
- Seventy-seven percent have less than three months' salary in savings, and 50 percent have zero in savings. That's one small emergency away from bankruptcy.

At least half the workforce admits to being stressed about their financial position. Financial stress, in fact, impacts many areas of our lives. One survey showed that 28 percent of employees say it affects their health, 23 percent say it affects their home relationships, 17 percent say it affects their work performance, and 8 percent say it even affects whether they attend work at all!

The Everyperson Test shows that all human beings essentially want the same things: to be healthy, happy, and financially secure. It stands to reason, therefore, that employers that make that easy and that help us achieve these life goals will enjoy loyalty, engagement, and extra effort from us in return.

Habits Make the Difference

The word "habits" sometimes gets a bad rap. People tend to think about habits as negative traits. You have a smoking habit or a habit of pro-crastinating or a habit of always being late or buying expensive lattes at your favorite coffee shop. But habits can also be powerfully positive. In our BRATLAB we have approached this issue from two angles. The first angle looks at research that supports a direct link between the good habits we practice and our health, happiness, and security. The second examines whether those habits can be directly linked to greater performance at work. Both approaches have proved fruitful.

Health and Performance

There is a wealth of research showing positive correlations between various aspects of healthy habits and performance. For example, stepping up your level of exercise improves not only your stamina (as you would expect) but also your cognitive function and emotional health. Sleeping better enables you to think and perform better, to make fewer mistakes, and to be less likely to be absent from work. Quit smoking and cognitive function improves and error rates go down eventually (although not initially). Just imagine how much better you'd perform being a nonsmoker who gets a good night's sleep and exercises.

Happiness and Performance

Be happy and you'll be more productive. Studies show that happiness is significantly linked with productivity, performance, and job satisfaction, with one study demonstrating a potential increase in productivity in the region of 40 percent. Positive emotions correlate with employees' sensitivity to opportunities, helpfulness to coworkers, confidence, cooperation, reduced aggressiveness, and increased persistence.

Positive mood can also boost attention, spur individuals to take action, and increase creative thinking ability. People with happy moods solve problems 20 percent more creatively when compared to people with neutral moods and 33 percent more compared to people with sad moods.

Security and Performance

When it comes to the connection between security and performance, almost all the research looks at the issue from the negative aspect. It focuses on reductions in performance or productivity losses linked to people's insecurity, especially financial insecurity. For example, research has shown that 25 percent of employees report decreased productivity due to financial stresses (and 50 percent admit taking time out of their workday to handle personal financial issues). Financial well-being, on the other hand, is positively correlated with workers' productivity. People with good financial wellness are mostly people who receive high performance ratings and rarely spend work time on personal financial issues.

The Common Factors

By and large, American workers are not healthy, happy, or secure. But why are these problems hidden, overlooked, or not successfully addressed? What are the root causes? Some of the reasons include (1) how we imagine the ideal employee should behave to get ahead;

(2) our failure to link health, happiness, and security to performance; (3) not knowing about or how to apply available habit creation research; and (4) the notion that we have to balance two separate lives—a work life and a home life. Let's address each in turn.

1. The Hero Archetype

What does the ideal go-getting employee look like? Many will tell you it's the hero archetype, the kind of employee who sacrifices him- or herself for the good of the company.

We put on a brave face and say we're working ourselves into an early grave, but are we more productive when we put in those extra hours, and do we owe it to the company to do so? We are visibly exhausted yet tell ourselves that this is proof that we're giving 110 percent. Employers and managers promote such employees and often exacerbate the problem by rewarding the "best" performers with even more work. In professions such as the law, medicine, and accounting, young employees are expected to suffer years of long nights, little sleep, and extreme stress to earn their stripes. Both managers and ambitious employees ignore the enormous impact this has on their quality of work and quality of life. We tell ourselves that we're toughening them up so they may succeed in their future careers.

In US hospitals, for instance, each year you'll find more than two million patients who are the victims of accidents that occur—*in the hospital*. About 440,000 die from errors made by doctors or nurses, and many of these cases can be blamed directly on inadequate sleep, too much stress, or a lack of concentration. Being unhealthy, unhappy, or insecure at work costs not only human lives but also millions of dollars in lost income, poor customer service, errors made, and other workplace blunders.

Some industries are acutely affected by these apparently heroic but costly sacrifices made by employees. At one extreme is the care business: home health care, hospice, nursing homes, and hospitals. By their very nature, many employees in these occupations find tremendous personal value in caring for others. Yet the hero archetype often leads to the almost perverse reality that some of these employees wear their own poor health, compassion fatigue, financial distress, or personal unhappiness as a badge of honor. It's something they have to live with for the privilege of helping others. At the other extreme, industries such as stock trading and management consulting, or company sales divisions, have a "work hard, play hard" culture. This, too, is often taken to the level where burnout is even expected: "If you're not dying, you're not trying."

Until we're able to change the narrative from "We serve our customers, companies, or children at the expense of ourselves" to "We serve our customers, companies, and children **by first** investing in ourselves," the value of health, happiness, and security to performance will remain obscured. Here's an example from our case files.

A Corporate Hero Transformation: Jay Kelley was a classic workaholic. More than nine years of long, grueling hours, a punishing travel schedule, stress, lack of sleep, and poor nutrition took their toll on his physical and mental health. The outcome of his lifestyle was adrenal and digestive issues, inflammation, and strained relationships. Then, just before his fortieth birthday, Jay accepted a position as president of Spire Labs, a social network that helps companies build healthy cultures and positive interactions in the workplace. It was a life-altering decision. The new work environment, with its commitment to health and fitness, was just what he needed. In addition, Jay watched his coworkers strive to become the best versions of themselves in all aspects of life, from the way they committed to exercise and heathy eating to the way they treated other people.

But it was their obsession with self-improvement that was the catalyst for Jay's three-year health journey. It began with a mutual love of soccer with his younger, faster peers and progressed to other physical activities. Physical fitness, of course, is one thing; mental fitness is another. And Jay acknowledges his biggest health breakthrough was an appreciation for mindfulness, which Jon Kabat-Zinn simply defines as paying attention on purpose and without judgment while being present in the moment. Two weeks after Jay was introduced to mindfulness meditation, his wife told him, "You are becoming a better version of you." Hearing that affirmation from the person closest to him was the game-changer in Jay's journey. Most important of all, he credits the changes he made with saving his marriage.

The support from his peers at Spire continues to keep Jay motivated and accountable. He eagerly pursues new endeavors, from rock climbing with his brother to mountain biking with his wife and sons. Result: he's become healthier and happier than ever and has significantly strengthened his relationships. He's thankful that the positive influences that came with his new job made it easy and natural for him to actually make the changes. And although the habits he focused on related to his happiness, health, and mental state, there was a business payoff: the most dramatic improvements were in his performance as a CEO.

2. Disconnected Data

Employers don't usually capture and analyze data that link worker health, happiness, and security to performance, at least not at an individual employee level. Ask employers about it and most point to their health insurance data, wellness program, and other human resource facts and figures. When pressed to show us their data on employee *performance* and not just costs or participation in programs, we find it rarely exists.

What about annual reviews? In our view, they're a very poor proxy for performance. More than anything else, ratings are influenced more by the relationship between the employee and the manager conducting the review. So what information is available?

Health: In the domain of health, hard information is often limited to health failures such as healthcare costs, disability claims, and absenteeism. Little, if any, data exist within employers to quantify positive attributes of health such as cardiovascular fitness, cognitive alertness, and low stress levels.

Happiness: Employee happiness is often gauged, at best, by surveys and, at worst, by complaint levels or exit interviews. Ironically, many employers spend more time discussing happiness with employees who quit instead of with those who stay. People are often assumed to be happy, until they leave.

Security: Data on employee security, especially financial security, are worst of all. Employers may know which benefits their employees participate in and the extent of their retirement fund contributions, but they almost never know about personal debt, student debt, and savings that employees have accumulated for either emergencies or retirement. In fact, many employees would tell employers that it's none of their business. The siloed nature of companies and privacy laws further complicate the matter. Employers are left in the dark and feeling like they are unable to help—assuming they were even inclined to try.

3. Unknown or Underutilized Research

The third reason why the value of health, happiness, and security is missed is that the research that has been done on how these factors drive performance is not widely known and understood by company leaders. In some cases, the research is discounted on the grounds that it was not conducted on their employees. In other cases, it is dismissed because it is based on employee self-reporting or interviews with employees or, for various other reasons, it is considered "soft and unreliable." In reality, there is more than sufficient evidence to make the case that healthy, happy, and secure employees significantly outperform those who are not.

4. The Myth of Work/Life Balance

Finally, the myth of work/life balance obscures the links between performance and health, happiness and security. The concept of work/life balance requires us to think of ourselves as two people: our work selves and our home selves. The concept is that while these two selves each have needs and wants and time that should be balanced, they should remain separated. But should that be the case?

Everyone seems to accept that work invades our home lives. It's quite natural for us to take home work that we did not complete at the office. Yet, it seems unacceptable that our home lives should invade our work space. Speaking to colleagues or managers about our health, personal finances, and relationships lies somewhere on the scale between awkward and inappropriate and even illegal (certainly in interview or hiring situations). We are understandably afraid that if we talk about our personal problems at work, we may be seen as weak or we might be fired or passed over for a promotion. So we all arrive at work each day, pretending to each other that everything at home is fine.

Until we create a culture in our workplaces that recognizes there is only one you, not a home you and a work you, the knowledge of what is really going on in our lives remains hidden. This robs us of not only the opportunity to understand the links between health, happiness, security, and performance but also the opportunity to support each other and our employees for our mutual benefit. Our humanity is being left at home when we head to work, and we all pay the price.

The solution is to identify and implement positive life-enhancing and business-building habits—habits that, as we shall see, create your destiny.

References

Aizer, A. (2010). The gender wage gap and domestic violence. *American Economic Review, 100*(4), 1847–1859. doi:10.1257/aer.100.4.1847

American Psychological Association (APA). (2007). Stress in America. Retrieved from http://www.apa.org/news/press/releases/2007/10/stress.aspx

APA. (2015). Stress in America: Paying with Our Health. Retrieved from https://www.apa.org/news/press/releases/stress/2014/stress-report.pdf

Blanchard, K. H., & Johnson, S. (1982). *The one minute manager.* New York: Morrow.

Bossidy, L., Charan, R., & Burck, C. (2002). *Execution: The discipline of getting things done.* New York: Crown Business.

Centers for Disease Control and Prevention (CDC). (2012). Summary health statistics for U.S. adults: National Health Interview Survey, 2010. *Vital and Health Statistics, 10*(252), 1–207.

CDC. (2006). State-specific prevalence of obesity among adults—United States, 2005. *MMWR, 55*(36), 985–988.

CDC. (2008). State-specific prevalence of obesity among adults—United States, 2007. *MMWR, 57*(28), 765–768.

CDC. (2010). Vital signs: State-specific prevalence of obesity among adults—United States, 2009. *MMWR, 59,* 1–5.

Central Intelligence Agency (CIA). The World Factbook Life Expectancy. Retrieved from https://www.cia.gov/library/publications/the-world-factbook/rankorder/2102rank.html

Ciccolo, J. T., Dunsiger, S. I., Williams, D. M., Bartholomew, J. B., Jennings, E. G., Ussher, M. H., Kraemer, W. J., & Marcus, B. H. (2011). Resistance training as an aid to standard smoking cessation treatment: a pilot study. *Nicotine and Tobacco Research, 13*(8), 756–760.

Clark, A., Fleche, S., Layard, R., Powdthavee, N., & Ward, G. (2018). *Origins of happiness: The science of well-being over the life course.* Princeton, NJ: Princeton University Press.

Clifton, J. (2017). Workplace disruption: From annual reviews to coaching. Retrieved from http://www.gallup.com/opinion/chairman/203876/workplace-disruption-annual-reviews-coaching.aspx?g_source=EMPLOYEE_ENGAGEMENT&g_medium=topic&g_campaign=tiles

Collins, J. C. (2001). *Good to great: Why some companies make the leap . . . and others don't.* New York: HarperBusiness.

Collins, J. C. (2009). *How the mighty fall: And why some companies never give in.* New York: Jim Collins.

Collins, J. C., & Hansen, M. T. (2011). *Great by choice—uncertainty, chaos, and luck: Why some thrive despite them all.* New York: HarperCollins.

Collins, J. C., & Porras, J. I. (1997). *Built to last: Successful habits of visionary companies.* New York: HarperBusiness.

Dew, J., Britt, S., & Huston, S. (2012). Examining the relationship between financial issues and divorce. *Family Relations, 61,* 615–628. doi:10.1111/j.1741-3729.2012.00715.x

Diener, E. (1984). Subjective well-being. *Psychological Bulletin, 95,* 542–575.

Diener, E., Suh, E. M., Lucas, R. E., & Smith, H. E. (1999). Subjective well-being: Three decades of progress. *Psychological Bulletin, 125,* 276–302.

Easton, J. F., Stephens, C. R., & Sicilia, H. R. (2017). An analysis of real, self-perceived, and desired BMI: Is there a need for regular screening to correct misperceptions and motivate weight reduction? *Frontiers in Public Health, 5,* 12. doi:10.3389/fpubh.2017.00012. Retrieved from http://journal.frontiersin.org/article/10.3389/fpubh.2017.00012

El Issa, E. (2016). 2016 American household credit card debt study. Retrieved from https://www.nerdwallet.com/blog/average-credit-card-debt-household/

Flegal, K. M., Carroll, M. D., Kit, B. K., & Ogden, C. L. (2012). Prevalence of obesity and trends in the distribution of body mass index among US adults, 1999–2010. *Journal of the American Medical Association, 307*(5), 491–497.

Gabler, N. (2016). The secret shame of middle-class Americans. Retrieved from https://www.theatlantic.com/magazine/archive/2016/05/my-secret-shame/476415/

Gallagher, M. W., Lopez, S. J., & Preacher, K. J. (2009). The hierarchical structure of well-being. *Journal of Personality, 77*(4). doi:10.1111/j.1467-6494.2009.00573.x

Garman, E. T. (2004). The importance of workplace financial education to employers. American Express Guide to Workplace Financial Education and Advice. Westerville, OH: Association for Financial Counseling and Planning Education (AFCPE).

Garman, E. T., Leech, I. E., & Grable, J. E. (1996). The negative impact of employee poor personal financial behaviors on employees. *Financial Counseling and Planning, 7,* 157–168.

Greenleaf, R. K. (1991). *The servant as leader.* Indianapolis, IN: Robert K. Greenleaf Center.

Habits at Work. (2014). *Dose value.* Chicago: BRATLAB.

Harrell, E., & Langton, L. (2012). Victims of identity theft, 2012. Office of Justice Programs, Bureau of Justice Statistics. Washington, DC: US Department of Justice.

Helliwell, J., Layard, R., & Sachs, J. (2016). *World happiness report 2016, update.* Vol. I. New York: Sustainable Development Solutions Network.

James, J. T. (2013). A new, evidence-based estimate of patient harms associated with hospital care. *Journal of Patient Safety, 9,* 122–128.

Johnson, A. (2013). 76% of Americans are living paycheck-to-paycheck. Retrieved from http://money.cnn.com/2013/06/24/pf/emergency-savings/

Kantor, E. D., Rehm, C. D., Haas, J. S., Chan, A. T., & Giovannucci, E. L. (2015). Trends in prescription drug use among adults in the United States from 1999–2012. *JAMA, 314*(17), 1818–1831.

Kelley, J. (2016). Letter to Andrew Sykes.

Keyes, C. L. M. (1998). Social well-being. *Social Psychology Quarterly, 61,* 121–140.

Kim, W. C., & Mauborgne, R. (2005). *Blue ocean strategy: How to create uncontested market space and make the competition irrelevant.* Boston: Harvard Business School Press.

Kolata, G. (2015). Death rates rising for middle-aged white Americans. *New York Times.* Retrieved from https://www.nytimes.com/2015/11/03/health/death-rates-rising-for-middle-aged-white-americans-study-finds.html?_r=0

La Montangne, C. (2013). NerdWallet Health finds medical bankruptcy accounts for majority of personal bankruptcies. Retrieved from https://www.nerdwallet.com/blog/health/managing-medical-bills/nerdwallet-health-study-estimates-56-million-americans-65-struggle-medical-bills-2013-2/

Loprinzi, P. D., Branscum, A., Hanks, J., & Smit, E. (2013). Healthy lifestyle characteristics and their joint association with cardiovascular disease biomarkers in US adults. *Mayo Clinic Proceedings, 91*(4), 432–442.

Lyubomirsky, S., King, L., & Diener, E. (2005). The benefits of frequent positive affect: Does happiness lead to success? *Psychological Bulletin, 131*(6), 803–855.

McGinnis, J. M., WilliamsRusso, P., & Knickman, J. R. (2002). The case for more active policy attention to health promotion. *Health Affairs, 21*(2), 78–93.

Merai, R., Siegel, C., Rakotz, M., Basch, P., Wright, J., Wong, B., & Thorpe, P. (2016). CDC Grand Rounds: A public health approach to detect and control hypertension. *MMWR, 65*(45), 1261–1264.

Moore, S. C., Patel, A. V., Matthews, C. E., Berrington de Gonzalez, A., Park, Y., Katki, H. A., et al. (2012). Leisure time physical activity of moderate to vigorous intensity and mortality: A large pooled cohort analysis. *PLoS Med, 9*(11), e1001335. doi:10.1371/journal.pmed.1001335. Retrieved from http://journals.plos.org/plosmedicine/article?id=10.1371/journal.pmed.1001335

National Center for Health Statistics. (2011). Health, United States, 2010: With special feature on death and dying. Table 95. Hyattsville, MD: National Center for Health Statistics.

Ogden, C. L., Carroll, M. D., Kit, B. K., & Flegal, K. M. (2012). Prevalence of obesity and trends in body mass index among US children and adolescents, 1999–2010. *Journal of the American Medical Association, 307*(5), 483–490.

Pilcher, J., Morris, D. M., Donnelly, J., & Feigl, H. B. (2015). Interactions between sleep habits and self-control. *Frontiers in Human Neuroscience, 9*, 284. doi:10.3389/fnhum.2015.00284. Retrieved from https://www.frontiersin.org/article/10.3389/fnhum.2015.00284

Porter, M. E. (1985). *The competitive advantage: Creating and sustaining superior performance.* New York: Free Press. (Republished with a new introduction, 1998.)

PricewaterhouseCoopers (PWC). (2016). Financial Wellness Survey. Retrieved from http://www.pwc.com/us/en/private-company-services/publications/financial-well-being-retirement-survey.html?icid=cs_us-hero-home_Financial-well-being-retirement-survey

Pratt, L. A., Brody, D. J., & Gu, Q. (2011). *Antidepressant use in persons aged 12 and over: United States, 2005–2008.* NCHS data brief, no. 76. Hyattsville, MD: National Center for Health Statistics.

Pyke, A. (2014). A third of Americans have almost nothing saved for retirement. Retrieved from http://thinkprogress.org/economy/2014/03/20/3416808/retirement-savings-survey/

Rowley, W. R., Bezold, C., Arikan, Y., Byrne, E., & Krohe, S. (2017). Diabetes 2030: Insights from yesterday, today, and future trends. *Population Health Management, 20*(1), 6–12. doi:10.1089/pop.2015.0181

Ryff, C. D. (1989). Happiness is everything, or is it? Explorations on the meaning of eudaimonic well-being. *Journal of Personality and Social Psychology, 57,* 1069–1081.

Ryff, C. D., & Keyes, C. L. M. (1995). The structure of eudaimonic well-being revisited. *Journal of Personality and Social Psychology, 69,* 719–727.

Ryff, C. D., & Singer, B. H. (2008). Know thyself and become what you are: A eudaimonic approach to psychological well-being. *Journal of Happiness Studies, 9,* 13–39.

Seiz, C. (2015). *Times of Trenton* guest opinion column.

United Nations. (2005–2010). UN World Population Prospects report, for 2005–2010. Retrieved from https://esa.un.org/unpd/wpp/

U.S. Department of Labor. (2017). American time survey. Bureau of Labor Statistics. Retrieved from https://www.bls.gov/tus/charts/

U.S. Department of Health and Human Services. President's Council on Fitness, Sports and Nutrition. Retrieved from https://www.fitness.gov/resource-center/facts-and-statistics/

Williams, O. (N.D.) How much is the average credit card debt in America? Retrieved from http://www.creditcards.com/credit-card-news/average-credit-card-debt.php

World Health Organization. (2013). World Health Statistics 2013. Retrieved from http://www.who.int/gho/publications/world_health_statistics/EN_WHS2013_Full.pdf

World Heart Federation Congress of Cardiology. (2012). Exercise helps smokers to quit smoking, to remain smoke-free and to reduce the risk of death. Retrieved from https://www.eurekalert.org/pub_releases/2012-04/whf-ehs041612.php

2

Habits Create
Your Destiny

Sow an act and you reap a habit.
Sow a habit and you reap a character.
Sow a character and you reap a destiny.

—Charles Reade, English novelist
and dramatist

Habits rule our lives—whether we like it or not, whether we know it or not. Even when they don't contribute positively to our lives, we find ways to excuse them. Before we explore the creation of positive habits that help us create our personal destinies and our company's destiny, let's start by looking at three common negative examples. We look at the way we rationalize a habit, the way we say "What the hell" as a road to continue indulging a habit, and the way we procrastinate instead of taking action today. Perhaps you'll recognize yourself. First, a personal confession from Andrew that highlights how easy it is to rationalize.

The Power of Rationalization

I smoked my first cigarette when I was just six years old, following an offer from my older brother to have a puff. From that point on, every few months my friends and I would sneak a cigarette or buy a pack from the local store (in those days, shopkeepers would sell cigarettes to kids sent to "buy them for their parents"). When I was in high school, I smoked regularly at parties and on weekends with friends. More of my friends smoked than those who did not, and by the time I was in college, it had become a regular habit of 10–20 cigarettes a day and a lot more on weekends or party nights.

I later qualified as an actuary, a profession extremely familiar with the grim statistics related to the impact of smoking on health and life span. As the youngest of eight children, with several of my siblings involved in the healthcare sector, I had no shortage of guidance about the danger of cigarettes. In fact, my sister had taken me to her medical school museum to see the black lungs and cancerous organs from patients who had died from lung cancer or other tobacco-related diseases. None of this made any difference to me.

For more than a decade, I ran a health insurance consulting business, and even then I continued to smoke. I drove from one meeting to the next, puffing away in the car, convincing myself that I did not reek of smoke during those meetings. I was clearly someone with a smoking habit. Yet if anyone had asked me, I would have denied being a smoker! Well, maybe I smoked, but I considered myself a social smoker. One who just happened to have a very active social life! For every plea from a family member or a friend, I had a ready answer to explain away my habit. In fact, my actuarial training had convinced me that the real risks of smoking mainly affected those over the age of 35. I had told myself that I would quit before then and rationalized that I could continue to smoke until then with little risk to my health. This is not true, of course, but such is the power we have to rationalize our habits to ourselves.

Despite this rationalization, by age 30, I really wanted to quit and had done so many times. After a long night of drinking and smoking, emboldened by a fresh hangover, I would swear off cigarettes, and since I could then go for days without smoking and without experiencing serious withdrawal effects, I was even more convinced that I didn't have a smoking habit. I was sure I could quit for good at any time. In reality, my off-again-on-again smoking habit lasted for more than 15 years of my adult life, with the longest periods of not smoking lasting only two years. There always seemed to be some reason that had me pick up "just one" cigarette again. Special occasions were often the cause or dating a new girlfriend who smoked. It didn't take much for me to slip back into being a 10–20-a-day smoker.

I can't remember the number of times that I said, "Just give me one puff," and ended up smoking for the next six months. When I finally did quit for good (and it has now been more than 10 years) and looked back on a lifetime of a gradually increasing smoking habit, it was littered with failed attempts at quitting. Something that I could do "any time I wanted" apparently had been much harder than it seemed. But it wasn't just that quitting itself is hard. What I noticed is how well and how often I had been the source of rationalizing stories to myself and others, which allowed me to continue to smoke. So now that we have dealt with rationalization, let's turn to the second negative habit—the temptation to say "What the hell."

The "What the Hell" Effect

Michele had been as skinny as a rake growing up and was sure she would never have to worry about being overweight. In fact, she looked down on people who were fat, writing them off as lacking willpower or being lazy. During college, though, she steadily gained weight. By the time she finished college, she'd gone beyond the so-called freshman 15 and piled on a total of 40 pounds. She knew it was her own fault. She'd been drinking and partying and staying up late at night to cram for finals and to finish term papers. And she pretty much lived on fast food. On the positive side, she played basketball four times a week, but the exercise was not enough to stop her gaining the weight.

After college, she landed her first job in PR, and the days were even longer than her time at college. She stopped playing sports ("Who has the time?") and ate up to three meals a day at the café inside her office building. By age 30, and just five and a half feet tall, she weighed in at over 250 pounds. She was no longer just overweight but obese and suffering other health problems. At her company's wellness day, her test results showed raised blood sugar indicative of diabetes, a cholesterol measurement that was through the roof, and elevated blood pressure. She could no longer climb a flight of stairs without having to stop on each landing to catch her breath. She had not been on a date in two years and spent most nights alone watching TV and comfort-eating ice cream and Doritos.

For the past two years, she had been seeing a therapist because she felt alone and depressed and sometimes had thoughts of killing herself. Her family had given up begging her to eat more healthily and exercise. She had tried more than 15 diets, and although she'd sometimes lost a few pounds, she always gained the weight back, and more. She had tried healthy meals from a weight-management company, but she hated the taste, and after just three days, she threw out the remainder of her month's supply. She felt that nothing would ever work, that she was just not the kind of person who could lose weight. She saw no point in even trying, when she was sure she would fail. She had resigned herself to continuing to gain weight and was afraid of losing her friends, family, and career as a result. She felt powerless and that her life was going over a cliff. Every time she tried to diet, she fell victim to the "What the hell" effect. When she did feel motivated to make a change, she could not help believing, "It won't be any different this time," and she would say to herself, "What the hell!" First coined by dieting researchers Janet Polivy and C. Peter Herman, the "What the hell" effect describes a cycle of indulgence, shame, and greater indulgence. These researchers noticed that many dieters would feel so bad about any lapse—a piece of pizza, a bite of cake—that they would say, "What the hell—I already blew my diet, so what's the point; I might as well eat the whole thing." As a result, for Michele, losing weight was not just hard but felt impossible.

So some of us rationalize our bad habits. Others shrug their shoulders and adopt the "What the hell" posture. And, for some, as we will see next, the culprit is the tendency to procrastinate.

Tomorrow Never Comes

When Keith had a stroke at age 53, the impact was devastating. He had been a successful, high-powered lawyer until that day but suddenly could barely speak or move, never mind practice law. As he slowly recovered, his gains in mobility and speech were marred by anxiety, anger, resentment, and worry for his family, who were suffering along with him as they faced financial upheaval.

By any standard, Keith had generated significant income. He'd become a partner in a large law firm in a record-breaking seven years and year after year had enjoyed salary increases—but his income always seemed to be swallowed up improving the lifestyle for his wife and two children. In fact, the more he earned, the more it seemed that he was on a treadmill of earning money just to keep up. By the time he was 35, they had moved out of the city to the suburbs and owned an enormous house (and mortgage), with two cars and a growing list of maintenance costs.

Keith was a smart guy. He knew that he should save for retirement and ensure that they had enough money for an emergency, but somehow there always seemed to be more pressing financial demands. And, of course, they needed to pay for exotic vacations, a boat on Lake Michigan, and a garage full of toys.

At age 40, Keith started his own practice, taking with him some marquee clients and immediately increasing his income. He didn't have an income problem. But he did have a spending habit, which was a problem. In the past three years Keith had earned more than $1 million each year, but it still wasn't enough to fund their lifestyle. He couldn't imagine how he could save for retirement. But he did have a plan—kind of. When the kids completed college and left home, he'd have more disposable income and would spend the final 10 years of his career saving for retirement. It was the same "plan" for buying life insurance, paying off his credit cards, and funding his kids' college funds: "I'll get to it soon, perhaps as soon as tomorrow." Sometimes he'd say to himself, "Next time I increase my hourly rate, I'll take the extra amount and put it into savings." But it never happened.

In contrast, Keith discovered that his friend and neighbor, David, was sitting pretty. Sure, David's house was not as big, he didn't have nice cars (in fact, the last time he'd bought a new car was more than 10 years earlier), and they vacationed in Florida at the same place each year. David was just a salaried employee, in the finance department of an unexciting local firm, yet he had $100,000 in emergency funds, his two daughters had more than $150,000 invested in their 529 college funds, and his 401(k) fund stood at more than $2 million. He was also more interested in insuring his life and the assets he already had than stepping up his lifestyle. His lifestyle just made no sense to Keith. That is, until he suffered a stroke.

While somewhat bolstered by the disability income insurance Keith's partner in his firm had purchased for them both (despite neglecting to update it for several years), Keith's income plummeted. He had been the rainmaker, and his business suffered from his absence. He was getting only one-tenth of what he'd earned and was under pressure from mounting uncovered medical bills. Within a year, his partner left the firm, and the business dissolved. Keith was unable to pay their mortgage and was forced to sell their house at a loss, barely getting enough to cover the outstanding mortgage, let alone make a dent in their credit card debt. Keith and his wife, Sharon, now live with her brother in Wisconsin, and she makes a contribution from the small salary she earns working at the local hair salon. Keith spends his days angry, frustrated, and worried, as they still face large debts. He knows they should declare bankruptcy, but his pride has so far prevented him from doing so. Keith learned what most of us learn too late: financial independence is not a problem of income—it's a habit problem.

It's Only Hard Because You Say It Is

These stories are of real situations that people have faced. They illustrate how we think about and act on challenges, habits, and situations that are a reality for many Americans. Many people are income rich and asset poor, although there are many more people who are income poor as well as asset poor. Millions of people wake up every day wishing they would exercise more, eat better, quit smoking, stop drinking alcohol or taking illegal drugs, or finally get around to organizing their financial affairs. Yet, for most people, tomorrow never comes, and the mountain to climb just seems too hard. Why is it so hard for the majority when there are others who are in good health, who do exercise each day, who thrive on their income, and who are well prepared for retirement and protected in the face of most emergencies?

There are people who seem happy and contented with their lives, who don't seem stressed or depressed, and who just seem to have it all together. They're the people who have created the habits to create their own preferred destiny. But why don't we see this link between our habits and who we become? What do we believe makes us who we are, instead?

Forging a Growth Mind-Set

Most people say a combination of their life experiences, their education, their family, and their upbringing make them who they are. Others point to their morals, their values, their religious faith, their genes, or even just dumb luck. An appealing explanation for exceptional performance is the concept of God-given, or natural, talents. Of course, all of the above have an influence on who and what we become, but we tend to overestimate how static or fixed we are as human beings.

Stanford University psychologist Carol Dweck, in her book *Mindset: The New Psychology of Success*, notes the differences between a fixed mind-set and a growth mind-set. People with a fixed mind-set, she says, believe that their basic qualities, such as their intelligence or talents, are cast in stone. They spend their time documenting their intelligence or talents instead of developing them. People with a growth mind-set, on the other hand, believe in expanding their most basic abilities through dedication and hard work; brains are just the starting point. This view creates a love of learning and a resilience that are essential for great accomplishment. Virtually all notably successful people have these qualities and the habits they help create.

As Malcolm Gladwell points out in *Outliers: The Story of Success*, exceptional performers are more likely to be those who have invested more than 10,000 hours of deliberate practice, honing their skill or craft. It is almost always a fallacy, he says, that some people are born great. Behind every apparent child prodigy, musical genius, or renaissance billionaire lie the multitude of hours they spent to achieve their brilliance.

We learn from Dweck and Gladwell that habits are at work. People with a growth mind-set forge good habits and reduce or remove poor habits. People who practice hour after hour are creating and fine-tuning their good habits. It's advice that carries through whatever your undertaking may be. For example, people who lose a lot of weight and keep it off often make a single small change, such as removing sugary soda from their diet or cutting out dessert. People get fit by taking the stairs instead of the elevator or leaving their car at the far end of a parking lot rather than immediately throwing themselves into training for a marathon. These small first steps lead to bigger gains over time as people's confidence and competence increase. Financially troubled individuals pay off small debts before tackling the big ones, and this snowball effect keeps them going and, over time, leads to their success.

The same logic applies to our performance at work. High-performing employees are not necessarily more talented, better educated, or better connected than low performers. Instead, they consistently practice a few high-performance habits that eventually compound into a significant difference in results.

You see tangible examples with salespeople. Let me give you an instance from our own organization. A young salesperson tasked with filling a seminar spent a few weeks doing background research, planning whom to call, and preparing phone scripts. He did everything except make the calls! Sure, that's the most daunting part, but nothing he'd done had true value until he could get into the single habit of picking up the phone and dialing. After a few conversations with him, in which he initially defended the worthiness of all the background research, I watched him have a quiet talk with himself, pumping himself up to make the calls. His first efforts were disasters. Calls went unanswered. Voicemails were not returned. When he did reach someone, he fumbled and mumbled through the script he had prepared. But he stuck with it, and within a few days he began to hone his skill at this new habit, and he successfully filled the room.

The simple difference: practicing and gaining mastery in the habit of making calls—just like Michael Jordan practicing free throws hour after hour after hour!

Habits Are Hobbits

Habits are a bit like Tolkien's mythological humanoids, the Hobbits: small and unappreciated. Their value is often underestimated because of their size. However, we argue that being small is actually a very good thing, because that means habits are also unnoticeable to others as your secret weapon. Habits are tiny acts, and each one on its own doesn't seem to make much difference. But when you think about it, habits are also very much like compound interest. If you put $100 in the bank today and come back tomorrow, you'll have about $100.01. Unimpressive. Even a year from now at an interest rate of 5 percent, you'll have only $105.00. But take a longer-term view, say 100 years, and then $100 in the bank earning "only" 5 percent a year will grow to be worth more than $13,000. Fortunately, we don't have to wait hundreds of years with habits, because the 5 percent improvements in our performance can be achieved in days and not years, as we work to improve the consistency and quality of our habits.

Consider that if, through deliberate practice, you get only 1 percent better each day (at, say, making sales calls), at the end of a 365-day year, this means you'll be 38 TIMES better! Even just allowing for a 220-day working year, a 1 percent daily improvement in the habit would make us nine times more effective in a single year. Ask yourself this: are you nine times better this year, at your job, than you were a year ago?

As we noted in the introduction, CEOs often say, "People are our most important asset." In fact, it's not our people but our people's (good) habits that are a company's most important asset. Ask any CEO or head of recruitment whether he or she has ever hired a superstar on paper only to discover that the person is actually a disaster (disa"star") in reality. Then sit back and listen to the horror stories! Why? Because as smart, educated, and experienced as superstars may appear to be, their bad habits get in their way or cause friction with others.

Habits Are Your DNA

Habits are also not considered sexy. They're not exciting when stacked against big corporate ideas such as strategy, vision, a venture capital injection of $100 million, or the newest management fad. But habits are the gene code of your company. They're present in each and every cell of the corporation (otherwise known as employees) and are expressed differently in each cell (so some employees express the habits of accountants, some express the habits of salespeople, and others express the habits of customer service agents).

When we watch a life form in action, we don't see the genes hard at work in every cell producing enzymes, proteins, and hormones and coordinating their actions to support working organs, moving limbs, thinking brains, and more. We see a living organism whose success is highly dependent on higher-level actions. In the same way, watching a business in action means that we see and appreciate strategy development, sales operations, funding, management processes, product development, and customer service. But we don't notice the "cellular-level" view of the individual habits that make up the role of each person that, when added together, comprise these higher-level functions or that create the visible markers of success.

When leaders say, "Excellence is in our DNA," what they're pointing to is the habits of their employees. Peter Drucker said that "culture eats strategy for breakfast," but what he didn't say, but perhaps should have, is that employee habits ARE your company culture. When we walk into a company and experience its culture, what we're experiencing is the things people say (verbal habits) and the way they behave (action habits) and even the way they think (mental habits). Culture is nothing more, or less, than the habits of leaders, managers, and employees.

Habits Are Focused

Finally, we hold onto myths that obscure the view of habits as the key drivers of performance. One such myth is the idea that we're good at multitasking and that our roles require us to be skilled at many things. It is true that many of us have varied roles, and we perform tasks that are quite diverse. In an office environment, for instance, they include holding and attending meetings, compiling reports and memos, sending emails, managing a team, and so on. But we often don't discriminate between what's truly important and stuff that seemingly needs to be done. We believe that if we're busy, we're effective. However, if we take a brutally honest view of each day and ask ourselves, "Which particular actions actually moved the business forward?" we might be unpleasantly surprised by the answer.

As a salesperson, sending an informational email to a prospect might be useful, but did it contribute to getting the sale? Think of the countless emails we transmit that don't snag results. Think of the numerous meetings we leave complaining about how much time we just wasted. Many of the actions we take each day make little difference in the end. We're just in the habit of doing them. But perhaps you disagree and feel that *everything* you do really matters. That's why We would like you to try this exercise before we move on:

1. Write down everything that you did yesterday—a list of tasks that you completed.
2. Write down what direct results you achieved through completing these tasks.

3. From that list of results achieved, try to put a monetary value on each—in terms not of the value of your time but of new revenue generated or money saved or value accrued to your business, from a shareholder's perspective.

4. Focus on the top three financial results that you produced from this list. Which tasks (from no. 1 above) delivered these results? For most people, the top three results comprise north of 80 percent of the value they add each day. Now estimate the time you took to produce these results. It's very unlikely to be more than two or three hours of your day.

This exercise indicates that you could potentially achieve 80 percent productivity in a day from performing two or three hours of work. Just imagine what you could do if you made better use of the remaining hours. We all know this intuitively, but we get sucked into poorly run meetings that often don't achieve anything valuable, feel obligated to reply to unnecessary emails (even if we are one of 30 people copied), and valiantly handle many other tasks that don't really contribute anything to the overall goals of our job or the value of our company. In other words, we all have many unproductive habits.

We're not the first people to take the view that habits are the genesis of performance. Stephen Covey's most famous book, *The 7 Habits of Highly Effective People*, was one of the pioneers. The difference between those who follow Covey's lead and that of this book is that they tend to think there are two elements that explain why some people are more successful than others. The first is the work itself, and the second is a set of habits that are overlaid on top of the actual work. We have a different view. We think it's habits all the way down. Your entire job can be defined in terms of habits. There is almost nothing that makes you effective that is **not** a habit.

Conversely, the things that rob us of our performance are habits too—just poor habits. There is almost nothing that you do just once that produces remarkable results, and there are also few time-wasting actions that you don't repeat again and again. Competence comes from repetitive *positive* actions that are improved upon each time and the avoidance of nonproductive habits. Experts are people who reliably produce high levels of performance in a given domain. They achieve this mastery by years of deliberate practice at the tasks—or habits—that define their expertise, whether that's playing basketball, playing the piano, speaking in public, or predicting earthquakes. Habits create your destiny. What you do every day matters more than what you do once in a while. All of your successes and failures come from the little actions, little decisions, and little moments that you perform on a daily basis.

So how do we distinguish between the habits that are effective and the ones that either waste time or make little difference? Which habits really make the difference to employee performance and to what degree? In the next chapter we will provide some answers with real-life examples from three totally different organizations with which we have worked.

References

Cave, A. (2017). Culture eats strategy for breakfast. So what's for lunch? *Forbes* magazine. Retrieved from https://www.forbes.com/sites/andrewcave/2017/11/09/culture-eats-strategy-for-breakfast-so-whats-for-lunch/#51bbe3697e0f

Covey, S. R. (2004). *The 7 habits of highly effective people: Restoring the character ethic* (Rev. ed.). New York: Free Press.

Dweck, C. S. (2008). *Mindset: The new psychology of success*. New York: Ballantine Books.

Gladwell, M. (2008). *Outliers: The story of success*. New York: Little, Brown and Company.

3

Habits That Matter

It's a matter of choosing what is most important to you and putting that first. Once you have recognized your true purpose in life, this becomes much easier.

—Clarence "The Big Man" Clemons, saxophonist and actor

What do the successes of a large public school district in Colorado, a small private advertising agency in Wisconsin, and a disruptive national hotel chain have in common? And what can senior corporate executives learn from their experiences?

First of all, each were led by a small group of people with a genuine vision for the future of their organization, which had more to do with the impact they could make than the money they could make (or save). Second, these leaders discovered two important secrets:

1. How to pinpoint the **right** employee habits to create a different future.
2. **How** to make it easy and natural for employees to practice these habits in the place where it matters the most: the workplace.

They were very clear that, for their organizations as a whole, employee **habits create your destiny**. So, before we go any further, let's examine these three examples.

School District's Healthy Turnaround

September 2008 was a dark month in American economic history. Fannie Mae and Freddie Mac were taken under government control, Bank of America purchased Merrill Lynch, and Lehman brothers filed for bankruptcy. AIG, the world's largest insurer, a company that was deemed "too big to fail," accepted $85 billion in federal bailouts, while regulators closed Washington Mutual Bank in the largest-ever US bank failure. Goldman Sachs, Morgan Stanley, and other once prestigious firms were vilified in the minds of Americans as greedy corporations that caused the worst global recession in living memory. Executives from Ford, GM, and Chrysler infamously flew into Washington, DC, in their corporate jets to plead poverty and request a bailout. Congress obliged to the tune of $700 billion.

All of this felt like a world apart as a group of leaders of the Douglas County School District (DCSD) in Castle Rock, south of Denver, met to discuss their own issues. DCSD was bursting at the seams. In 15 years, it had grown by more than 40,000 students to a total of almost 60,000 students in a community of 250,000 residents. New schools had to be built, programs and services expanded, and an increasingly expensive set of employee health benefits funded. The self-funded health plan was $2 million in the red, projected to lose

$4 million in the coming year. A broken health insurance system was partly to blame for the burgeoning costs, but so were the deteriorating health of employees and their disinterest in the wellness programs on offer. In fact, in 2008, only 11 out of 7,000 employees had completed the insurer's health risk assessment!

The district was confident, however, that this dilemma would be resolved by a $500-million boost from an increase in property taxes, part of a significant bond and budget vote in the upcoming general election. On November 5, 2008, the election results were in: Barack Obama celebrated his victory as the first African American president of the United States, but the leaders of the Douglas County School District were despondent in defeat. They had lost their vote by a 4 percent margin. Days later, the bad news was compounded with the realization that state funding for school districts would be severely cut not only in 2009 but also, quite probably, for several years to come. As the financial crisis spread from Wall Street to Main Street, by February 2009 the implications for the school district were painfully clear: nearly 300 jobs eliminated, employee pay frozen, and furlough days introduced (unpaid, forced "vacation days"). Class sizes increased, and all but core programs were slashed.

Something had to be done. In partnership with the district, we created Health Matters, a healthy habits strategy to cut costs without cutting services and, at the same time, improve employee well-being. Teachers, though, were understandably resistant. When we talked with them, they were quick to point out that they'd already suffered frozen salaries, increased class sizes, and removal of programs. They were already being asked to do more with less. And now—*a wellness program*? Their reaction, in effect, was, "Now you want us to do one more thing. And what we hear you say is that we're sick, we're fat, we're diabetic, and we're expensive. And yet we have to participate in a program so that you can reduce the district's health care costs. What more do you want?" It was, at first blush, a disheartening, disempowering message. All the teachers really cared about was the reason they'd become teachers in the first place: their passion to educate the next generation. They hadn't signed up for this.

Assistant Superintendent Steve Herzog and his team took on the task of making the quest an inspirational one. They highlighted the fact that children who exercise get 20 percent better grades in English and math and other subjects, and they emphasized that teachers who have more stamina make better decisions and fewer errors. Most important of all—kids do what teachers do, not what teachers tell them to do! The plea: if not for the sake of your own health, be a role model for the kids. The old message was "We want you to participate for your own health and to help us reduce health insurance costs." The new message became "We NEED you to participate, as role models for your students. Healthy teachers teaching healthy kids results in better grades."

This message hit the spot, and within two months, more than 4,000 teachers and administrators went for it and signed up to champion the cause. "It was a shifting in mind-set of what was important," Brian Ewert, director of human resources, told me. Remember that in the prior year when times were good, only 11 people had participated.

Inspired teachers recruited and coached many of the 60,000 students not only to improve their own health but also to take it a step beyond by inviting the kids to become agents of change and role models for their parents. That was the magic that made the program work. It was a switch from the "What's in it for me?" mind-set to discovering meaning and value in life by motivating others.

Despite the fact that employees were the first in any Colorado school district to be asked to accept very high deductible health plans, their feedback was overwhelmingly positive because of the benefits that ensued from making health and wellness a priority. Even the bus drivers, a group of employees not easily excitable, became enthusiastic. One wrote, "After all the negatives, job layoffs, and stressful meetings, it is so nice to have this for a pick-me-up. This program is a day brightener for many of us—thank you."

And on top of all that came impressive financial results. Within two years, the district went from $2 million in the red to $2 million in the black on its self-funded health plan, and employees accrued more than $6 million in personal health savings accounts funded by the district.

DCSD had overcome some of its immediate financial crises, although many challenges lie ahead. The mood had dramatically changed from just 12 months before, when all seemed lost. Now, the pathway to financial survival, healthy teachers, improved student grades, and a stellar reputation as a growing school district was clear—all through the introduction of better habits. And guess what? Those habits were nothing extreme. To a large extent, the healthier habits were not much more than regular small chunks of exercise throughout the school day—a two-minute workout at the beginning of each class. As we said before, tiny habits can add up to big results!

Ad Agency Reinvents Itself and Gains Clients

Arketype Inc. was in many ways a typical small advertising agency. Its 30-member team worked extremely long hours, often pulling all-nighters, and they took pride in their work ethic despite the negative impact on them and their families. Watercooler conversation often focused on their stress and lack of sleep and how they coped with the pressure.

Jim Rivett, CEO of the Green Bay, Wisconsin, firm at the time, was concerned about the mental and physical health of his employees. But when he wanted to do something about it, he ran into a typical barrier: the employees wore their sacrifice as a badge of honor. It earned them bragging rights. And, anyway, they wanted to know, where could they find time to care for themselves when they needed to spend so much time meeting the demands of their clients?

On a chilly winter morning, Jim gathered the team together in their office, a rehabilitated downtown church, to discuss the challenges. He overcame the client satisfaction barrier by pointing out that clients would probably prefer to have creative ideas from a team that was full of life and vigor at 11:00 a.m. rather than ideas from a team that was tired and stressed out at 11:00 p.m. And then he overcame the time barrier when he was struck by the thought: "What would it be like if our offices became *the* place where people could spend time with their family and nurture their own health?"

In other words, if they couldn't find the time and the place to go to exercise, bring exercise to them. There wasn't a budget, but they had a wealth of creative minds who accepted this challenge as a design problem. Together, they quickly carved out a plan. One by one the employees spoke about the exercise equipment they had at home, stored under a bed or gathering dust in a garage. There was more than enough to fashion a highly functional gym in the office basement, instead of leaving it to rot at home. One Saturday, a month later, employees and family members cleaned out the basement, laid down donated rubber floor mats, and installed not only the gym equipment but also a kitchen. They celebrated with a healthy potluck dinner and brainstormed implementation of their new healthy habits regimen.

One team took on the task of creating walking paths—inside and outside the office—and soon walking meetings became a standard for project discussions. A second team arranged a health fair, including fitness tests, personal training sessions, and the participation of a local hospital. They also started a healthy living book club.

A third team developed a newspaper advertisement throwing down the gauntlet, urging other companies to follow their example.

Although long nights didn't completely disappear, the addition of healthy habits and mutual support improved work performance. One of the teams documented their journey in a short video that we still show during keynotes today. And there was a surprising business bonus from the newspaper ad. Two large healthcare companies took up the challenge to compete for healthiest company in Green Bay. As a direct result of this good press, Arketype was invited to bid on—and won—advertising business in the healthcare industry, where they had not operated before. The reason? Healthcare companies wanted their advertising created by a team that was aligned with their own brand's health position.

Jim went on to found a new agency, but the Arketype adventure and his own personal health journey live with him to this day. What really struck him was the effect it had on people as individuals. In one instance, the initiative even helped identify and successfully resolve an employee's life-threatening condition. Says Jim, "My first reaction was, Wow! This is impacting people in ways I never imagined. What if we never had the foresight and trust to create an innovative solution just because we did not have the financial means to do so? Talk about creativity!"

Kimpton Hotels' Life-Changing Habits

A goldfish bowl, throwing pumpkins off a roof, and animal-print bathrobes. How could they possibly be linked? The answer is Kimpton Hotels and Restaurants. And company founder Bill Kimpton.

More than three decades ago, Bill disrupted the hotel industry when he scorned the large and impersonal design of traditional hotels and introduced the boutique hotel, a stylish home away from home. It was a groundbreaking idea and not without its risks. In fact, the business was touch-and-go for a while, and Steve Pinetti, one of the cofounders and senior vice president, even saved costs by living in the hotel. Serendipitously, it proved to be the best move he could have made because, while living there, he realized that the value of decisions made by the corporate owners paled in significance compared with the small daily actions of frontline employees, when it came to the guest experience.

It led Steve to forge a thriving culture focused on empowered employees, in which negative habits were replaced with positive habits. Kimpton offers its employees extreme autonomy, and it rewards innovation. Moreover, innovation is not only encouraged but also expected. And that's where the goldfish, the pumpkin, and the animal-print bathrobes play a starring role.

The idea of placing a goldfish in a bowl in every room of the Kimpton Hotels' Monaco brand came from a member of the housekeeping team. The thinking is that it's soothing to watch a goldfish swimming around, and it reminds you of being at home. However, just imagine what it must feel like to be a housekeeping employee who not only dreams up such an idea but also sees it executed room after room. That's one of the reasons why Kimpton Hotels is consistently rated as a best place to work.

The pumpkins? How about a corporate sales event where guests, instead of idly standing around sipping wine and nibbling cheese, get to throw pumpkins off the roof aimed at a target on the ground below? That's much more fun and engaging. More importantly, this kind of creativity is how hotel managers at Kimpton deliver on their promise to "fill every bed every night." They find new and creative ways to market their hotel to local companies, and this helps explain why they have higher than average occupancy and the greatest ROI of any hotel group over the period of its existence.

And the animal-print bathrobes? That was another employee idea based on the assumption that every woman has (or secretly wants) an animal-print item of clothing. The bathrobe contributes to the comforting feel of being at home. While other hotels' managers complain that bathrobes get stolen, Kimpton Hotel managers celebrate selling a lot of these bathrobes. Every few years customers and employees participate in a photo competition, with the winners sending in photos wearing the robes in the most exotic places (like on the Great Wall of China). It may seem like a small thing, but this is how brand loyalty is built.

No wonder the Kimpton Hotels & Restaurants group has been recognized by top publications for its superb customer satisfaction, including being named *U.S. News & World Report*'s Best Hotel in the USA and repeatedly listed as one of *FORTUNE*'s 100 Best Companies to Work For. Most notably, Kimpton is known for having the lowest staff turnover in the industry. According to Steve Pinetti, it's due to the employee-centric culture that Bill Kimpton inspired. Also expected is that every employee, from leadership to housekeeping, goes "out of bounds to fix a problem."

Kimpton believes that happy employees lead to happy guests and that happy guests lead to a thriving hotel business. Company leaders continually ask, "What can we do to make our employees happy?" As a result, employees are offered phenomenal benefits, including pet insurance, paid volunteer days, tuition reimbursement, bereavement leave, a benefits help desk (that actually goes out of its way to help employees understand benefits issues), a food truck service, and much more. Kimpton wants employees who are challenged, who have a purpose and meaning in their lives, and who have healthy relationships at work and at home. For them, being happy includes growing, learning, innovating, and serving others. Perhaps most important, it means open communication in a high-trust environment.

How does a company this large and diverse build and maintain this level of trust and communication? Through company-wide training sessions at which Pinetti helps employees recognize the ruts and routines (the habits) that inhibit them. Whether those ruts include hitting the snooze button in the morning or repeating the same, mindless actions each day (like answering emails with no thought to which ones are most important), he makes employees aware of how these habits shape not only their days but also their lives. He pushes them to create new habits, to take risks, and to find solutions that not only make them happier but also more productive. One of Pinetti's sessions asks employees to populate a seven-day calendar, which includes a date night, free time, exercise sessions, or anything else they want to add, and then asks them to commit to living according to that calendar for at least two weeks. Then they participate in open discussion, shared triumphs, and regular check-ins for accountability, which are all keys to success. In just two weeks, he sees amazing changes in not only people's routines and habits but also their performance.

These sessions break down company hierarchy and build trust. "All employees have a direct line to the highest people in the company, and no one is afraid to talk to anybody about anything," says Pinetti. "If you can think it, we can do it." The trust that is built during these sessions enables employees at all levels to act with autonomy. The message: it's better to try something new and fail than not try at all. It's a message that has become a pillar of Kimpton company culture.

Knowing that you can't control the competition, Pinetti uses his employees as his competitive advantage. He does this by investing in the personal and professional habits that future-proof their business, and that mobilizes innovation in the very moment when customers interact with employees. It's a far cry from the common top-down approach, when a bright idea from a head office team is rolled out months—maybe even years—after being developed, if at all. Innovation in Kimpton hotels is tried, tested, and proved one customer at a time and then scaled. That, more than anything else, is what makes the company a formidable competitor and a pleasure to visit as a customer.

You may have missed the little habit that makes all the difference. Steve inspires all employees to practice the habit of asking themselves, "What's the one thing I can do, right now, to make THIS guest's experience awesome?" It's this question that leads to the animal-print bath robes, the pumpkin-smashing event, and the goldfish in the room, as well as hundreds of great experiences from guests that worked for them, in that moment, but that never needed to become a brand standard. This one question, a mental habit, allows Kimpton to provide unique experiences, at scale. If you choose the right employee habits, they can scale a singularly unique experience for your customers, instead of mandating a cookie-cutter approach to customer service. The difference it creates is the difference you feel when you eat at an artisanal burger joint with a unique and interesting menu, compared with just another chain burger restaurant.

The other habit that is hidden from view is the Kimpton Hotel manager's habits of saying yes, even in the face of risk. Most companies' managers are trained to say NO and to say it often. That's one of the reasons why so many employees are disengaged and why they keep their ideas to themselves. A risk-averse management culture kills creativity. But Kimpton was able to see that the biggest risk of all that it faces is the risk of offering guests a mediocre experience, like so many other hotels that have tried to put in place a one-size-fits-all approach to customer service. Managers who have the habit of saying yes to new experiments leave employees feeling inspired, and, even when the experiments don't work, most guests are at least touched by the personal effort to create a unique experience.

Here's the key takeaway: the small habits of employees and managers at Kimpton Hotels are almost impossible to see from the outside and therefore difficult to copy. This provides them with a sustainable competitive advantage. There have been many companies that have jumped on the bandwagon of creating boutique hotels but none that match the Kimpton promise of an awesome and unique experience every time you visit one of its hotels.

So let's recap: the school district, the advertising agency, and the hotel chain all empowered their most valuable asset: their people's good habits. They replaced their bad habits with high-performance habits. It was a team effort. And none of the changes in habits were so dramatic that they became a turn-off. Instead, they quickly became a catalyst. If you or your CEOs still believe that "people are our most important asset," we challenge to you consider our view that "it's your people's (good) habits that are your most important asset." However, supporting employees in creating these habits—not only their work habits but also the ones that help them to live big and fulfilling lives—requires that you genuinely care about them as people. If you do, the results can transform your organization. In the pages that follow, we will begin with delving deeper into the habits that matter most, and, in subsequent chapters, we will then look at how to design your company to make them a reality.

There are two distinct types of habits that must be discovered and adopted to boost employee performance: Work Habits and Pivotal Performance Habits. We must understand the role of both before we proceed to discover the impact they can have in creating high-performance companies.

Work Habits

The fundamental unit of corporate competitive advantage is having your employees at every level practice a small set of habits every day,

day after day. Competence in one's role comes from gaining mastery of the habits that make up each person's position, whether it is creating new products, managing people, machining widgets, servicing customers, making sales, or virtually every other function.

As a salesperson, for instance, these Work Habits might include making cold calls, updating sales management software, sending proposals, crafting compelling presentations, asking for the deal, and ensuring contracts get signed. These Work Habits are unique to a particular role in a company. Some of the habits of effective salespeople match those of effective accountants, of course: things such as asking great questions, listening well, and being on time. You can refer to a list of these ten high performance habits in chapter 10, Putting It All Together. But for accountants, their set of effective Work Habits might include balancing the company accounts each month, issuing invoices, collecting outstanding payments, paying creditors, and producing monthly financial statements. The employees' destiny—career path success (or failure)—is almost entirely determined by the work habits that they practice (both the good ones and the bad ones). In fact, practicing these Work Habits defines what it means to do a good job.

Pivotal Performance Habits

Pivotal Performance Habits **prepare us to perform** our Work Habits. These are the habits that ensure that we show up at work each day full of energy, mentally sharp, and confident. They are habits that leave us highly engaged with our work and our customers and inspired to make a difference; habits that ensure we're well rested and able to make rapid and good decisions and minimize our mistakes; habits that ensure we're not worried about our lives outside of work, specifically, how we're going to make ends meet this month, or avoid creditors, or deal with an unhappy home situation. Habits that prepare us to perform are like a motor that turns the wheel of our ability to complete the habits that make up our individual roles in our company.

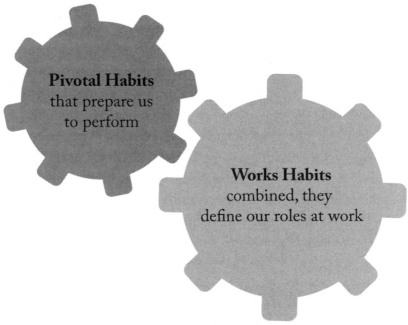

Pivotal Habits that prepare us to perform

Works Habits combined, they define our roles at work

Figure 3.1: Pivotal Habits are the primary cog that powerfully turns the cog of Work Habits.

These habits that prepare us to perform can have a profound impact across a business because:

a) They significantly improve our ability to practice our Work Habits with greater accuracy, speed, stamina, and quality, and they enable us to do them at lower costs (in terms of health-related costs and benefits, time off, or periods of low productivity).

b) They apply to every single person in the company. Although many of our Work Habits are unique to our specific roles, the habits that prepare us to perform are common to **every** employee and enable the whole cohort of employees to operate at the highest level.

c) They are habits that employers have traditionally ignored, failed at cultivating in their employees, and have not approached as a design problem. This is a missed opportunity to elevate the performance of the whole company, and, because most employers miss the crucial role of these preparatory performance habits, it also provides a difficult-to-copy competitive advantage for employers.

DEFINITION: WORK HABITS: the repetitive actions that make up our job roles and that, if practiced with increasing fidelity over time, explain our personal job performance at work. Work Habits of individuals or teams together make up higher-level drivers of competitive advantage such as leadership, management, execution, strategy development, innovation, product development, and essentially all the drivers of sustainable corporate performance. For a list of these common habits, refer to chapter 10.

DEFINITION: PIVOTAL HABITS: the repetitive actions that prepare us to perform, in life and at work, by ensuring that we have the energy, mental clarity, stamina, and freedom from health, financial, relationship, or other concerns that can distract us from performing. Pivotal Habits are the primary cog in the machine that powerfully turns the cog of Work Habits. They are thus the foundation of not only human performance but also corporate performance. Pivotal Habits boil down to the set of habits that prepare us to perform, by helping employees get what they really want for themselves and their lives. Remember the Everyperson Test from chapter 1? Pivotal Habits help employees to be healthy, happy, and secure.

The BRATLAB Research

We created the Behavioral Research Applied Research Laboratory (BRATLAB) to answer four key questions.

1. Why have efforts at employee health, happiness, and security largely failed?
2. Which habits really matter when creating health, happiness, and security and for driving high levels of performance, and to what degree do these habits matter?
3. How do you effectively support people in practicing the right habits, in a way that leaves them highly engaged with their employer, thrilled by the experience, and grateful for the support they received?
4. What financial value can employers expect from a successful investment in supporting the right performance habits in their employees?

The bottom line: practicing the habits that most powerfully create healthy, happy, and secure employees drives high performance in both their personal lives and their work. It's a win for employers and for employees. But what are those habits, and how do they rank against each other?

Prescribing Habits

To rank the effectiveness of different habits, on different desired outcomes, our solution was to develop the concept of a **Dose Value**, borrowing the practice from the pharmaceutical industry. When you have a headache, for example, and you are in the pharmacy aisle staring at 30 different pain relief medications, you care about answers to questions like:

- Which drug will work best to relieve my headache?
- Which one will work the fastest or last the longest?
- How long will I have to take it before the pain diminishes?
- What are the possible side effects and costs?

Once you have answers to these questions, you can make an informed choice.

Similarly, a CEO with a "headache"—let's say unhappy and disengaged employees—will want to know which employee habits will work best to solve this problem. The CEO should ask questions like:

- Which habits work best to improve relationships at work?
- Which habits work best to improve perceived autonomy?
- Which habits work best to help people find meaning and purpose?
- Which habits work best to improve how happy someone feels at any given time?

Whatever "dose" of a given habit is chosen is the "prescription" for a particular habit. For example, four minutes of exercise every two hours might be the right dose to reduce error rates during the day. That "four minutes of exercise every two hours" is the prescription. Think of the prescription as the advice your performance "doctor" would give you if you asked him or her how to do better at your job or in life!

DEFINITION: the Dose Value is a description of the relationship between a habit and the value of the outcome that someone will enjoy from practicing that habit.

The Goldilocks Principle Applied to the Dose Value

Many habits have a point at which additional time, intensity, or frequency produces only limited additional gains or even incurs a decreasing result. Over-exercising, for example, can damage your health. When we review the research, we don't look for the point at which one is likely to achieve the maximum gain. Rather, we look for the optimal point, where you gain the most outcome value for the minimum amount of time and effort. We've all got lots to do in life, so we're looking for that sweet spot where we get the most value for the smallest investment. That's the "just right" level that most people are seeking, and so we call it the Goldilocks Habit Prescription—the least amount of change for the most significant outcome.

Why is it important to find this optimal level for each habit? You've probably heard people ask whether the best time to exercise is morning or evening. While some research suggests that morning is best, the accurate answer is "whenever you'll do it!" This highlights the fact that finding a way to fit habits into people's busy lives is critical if we are serious about wanting people to accomplish anything. The less time that needs to be invested and the easier it is, the better. The Goldilocks Habit Prescriptions are focused not only on the right amount of time and energy invested but also on how doable each habit is.

The List of Pivotal Habits

The table below lists the pivotal habits that we suggest people practice, based on BRATLAB research, to improve outcomes in the domains of health, happiness, and security. Few of the habits in this list will surprise you. However, they are the habits that our extensive research has shown provide most of the kinds of outcomes that CEOs and employees say they want, for themselves and for their businesses.

Health	Happiness	Security
Move	**Savor**	**Protect**
• *Exercise frequently* • *Stand and move more*	• *Savor positive experiences* • *Practice optimism* • *Express gratitude*	• *Purchase sufficient insurance* • *Protect against identity theft and fraud*
Nourish	**Focus**	**Manage**
• *Eat for optimal health and performance* • *Moderate consumption of coffee, alcohol, and sugar* • *Eliminate toxins* • *Supplement when appropriate*	• *Create positive relationships* • *Perform acts of kindness and generosity* • *Practice mindfulness*	• *Learn and apply money management skills* • *Reduce debt* • *Create a budget and track spending regularly*
Restore	**Foster**	**Save**
• *Sleep 7 to 8.5 hours per night* • *Limit device and screen usage* • *Manage stress* • *Take medication when medically advised*	• *Use character strengths* • *Show self-compassion* • *Live purposefully*	• *Save for retirement* • *Create and implement a short-term savings plan*

Deciding Which Habits to Practice: The Role of the Dose Value

The table above includes a lot of different habits, and so it becomes an important question to decide which one, or which ones, to practice at all and where to start. Our research enables us to help people and employers decide which habits to work on, given the outcomes THEY wish to achieve. It is far from a one-size-fits-all strategy!

You probably won't be surprised to hear that in the past we have found that most budget-conscious employers will say that they want programs that offer something for everyone. As appealing as these programs may appear in marketing materials for new recruits (and certainly to the CFO), the reality is that most broad programs are also very shallow. When it comes to seeing a return on investment, employers are much better served by doing one thing well, rather than many things poorly. The same rule applies to humans tackling new habits. In fact, we have a golden rule when it comes to creating new habits: we can create (or quit) only one habit at a time. So deciding which ONE habit to tackle, as a person and even as a company, is an important decision.

To illustrate, if an employer could focus on only one employee health habit, we would recommend that it choose exercise. Exercise not only has the highest Dose Value for a range of desired outcomes compared to the other health habits but also it is the "first domino" that makes it easier for many people to tackle, or knock over, other health habits. Rather than trying to get employees to quit smoking AND eat healthily AND improve their sleep all at the same time, employers are more likely to succeed if they help employees tackle one habit at a time, starting with the most important and creating a domino effect as a result.

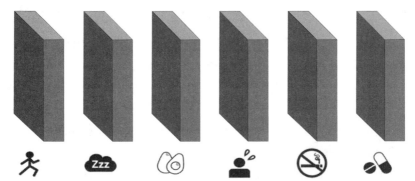

Figure 3.2: First domino effect: Employers are more likely to succeed if they help employees tackle one habit at a time, starting with the most important and creating a domino effect.

Having said that, for some employees, the best habit to start with might be something other than exercise. Either for psychological or practical reasons, they may be better served by starting with meditation. But the same rule applies: success is more likely if you tackle only one habit at a time, AND that habit should be something that you'll likely succeed at and that has a higher Dose Value for the things YOU care about.

Let's turn once again to our three key domains of health, happiness, and security to see how our Dose Value research, the single-habit focus, and the domino approach can be brought to life.

Health

An example of this domino effect is that people who exercise sleep better and have better appetite control. They also exhibit improved willpower, enabling them to make better food choices. Exercise increases our energy and lowers our stress levels. There is a strong correlation between those people who exercise and those who don't smoke. It's reported that as few as 6 percent of the fittest people smoke, compared with as many as 25 percent of the least fit.

Overall, there is a wealth of research showing the positive impact of exercise on various aspects of costs and performance at work:

Costs
- Being physically active leads to 24 percent lower healthcare costs.
- Participation in physical activity reduces risk of depression.
- Walking 30 minutes a day reduces tension and anxiety.
- Being physically active leads to a 24 percent reduction in sick leave absence.
- Exercising vigorously three times a week reduces sick leave days by 19 percent.

Performance

- A combined exercise program of at least six months improves cognitive function by 34 percent.
- Fit individuals make 10 percent fewer inhibition errors than the unfit at rest. Twenty minutes of exercise can beneficially impact error rates in the unfit.
- Ten minutes of exercise during the workday reduces mental fatigue by 26 percent and increases energy by 37 percent.
- Exercise during work hours increases units per man-hour (or average production rate) by 9 percent.
- Exercising at a moderate level of intensity for at least 30 minutes improves decision-making immediately following exercise, up to 60 minutes after exercise.
- Intense physical activity results in 20 percent faster learning immediately following exercise and improves long-term retention over sedentary or moderate exercisers.

Based on the relative strength of the Dose Value of each habit, we recommend that people tackle health habits in this order:

1. Exercise regularly
2. Manage stress
3. Eat healthily
4. Practice sleep habits
5. Quit smoking

As we mentioned above, for some people there may be good personal reasons to tackle these habits in a different order.

Happiness

Much like exercise, the habits that increase happiness seem to have strong positive correlation with increases in productivity:

- Practicing mindfulness regularly is correlated with around 30–50 percent fewer errors, a 50 percent increase in energy levels, and a 56 percent decrease in emotional exhaustion.
- People who are happy are 35 percent more likely to take action.
- Employees with high positive well-being have 40 percent higher productivity.
- Having high levels of happiness leads to around a 20 percent increase in stamina.

Based on the relative strength of the Dose Value of each habit across the range of desirable outcomes, we recommend that people tackle happiness habits in this order:

1. Practice mindfulness
2. Express gratitude
3. Savor positive experiences
4. Use signature strengths
5. Perform acts of kindness

Security

Unlike the domain of health, where exercise produces an across-the-board impact, in the domain of financial security, habits have a more direct—and painfully obvious—relationship with each outcome. To retire comfortably, the key habit is to save more for retirement. To reduce debt, the key habit is to pay off debt. However, just as exercise can be considered the first health domino, and mindfulness the first happiness domino, some financial security habits should be considered before others, as they may make the entire journey of habits easier to start and to complete.

In this domain, we align strongly with financial guru Dave Ramsey, who has helped millions of people gain financial security.

He advocates beginning with the small goal of saving $1,000, even before paying off a dollar of debt. That's because it is a relatively easy task for most people, which can be achieved in a few months, and provides a psychological boost and security from emergencies as they eliminate debt. The next step, he recommends, is paying off debts When it comes to paying off debt, start with the smallest outstanding debt you have, regardless of the interest rate, and knock off debts one by one. This too builds psychological confidence through a series of small wins that predicts ultimate success. Then Ramsey recommends increasing the emergency fund to three to six months of expenses—what it would take to pay your bills if you didn't have an income. Only then does he suggest investing for retirement, starting investments for college funding, paying off your mortgage, investing for wealth, and giving on a lavish level. Through all of these steps Ramsey recommends having the appropriate life insurance, health insurance, and insurance to protect your major assets such as home and auto.

We recommend that people tackle security habits in this order:

1. Reduce debt
2. Increase savings (short-term and/or retirement)
3. Protect your assets (health, life, real assets)

Bringing Pivotal Habits to Life, for Performance at Work

When considering the habits outlined above, a typical habit prescription for increased productivity at work might look like this:

Open or close each workday with 10 minutes of mindfulness practice. This could include traditional meditation, a walk, breathing exercises, or a couple of yoga postures or stretches. The overall effect of this will be a reduction in error rates, lower burnout, less emotional exhaustion, and an increase in energy and stamina.

Then add four minutes of high-intensity exercise every two hours. This not only has general positive health benefits and helps with stress reduction but also improves decision-making, learning, and memory.

Both the prescriptions above can quite easily be built into almost any workday and type of job, from the factory floor to the C-suite.

Finally, we would add managing finances more effectively by reducing debt, having adequate insurance, and increasing savings where possible. These habits can often be set up to be automatic (by designing them into the benefits offering of a company), and the benefit would be a significant reduction in employee stress and the associated costs and lost productivity. Struggling with finances as a result of bad financial habits is one of the major sources of stress.

Knowing which habits to practice and to what degree is the main objective of our Dose Value research. In the next chapter we will look more closely at the other critical element: designing the contexts of work to make it easier for people to practice these habits.

The Machinery of High-Performance Employers

The graphic below summarizes the "machinery" of high-performance employers. When employees practice a defined set of Pivotal Habits, they become healthy, happy, and secure (or at least more so than they were). When combined, these three outcomes lead to employees thriving in life and at work. Thriving employees have the energy, stamina, engagement, motivation, and mental ability to effectively perform the Work Habits that make up their job roles. And it is these Work Habits (See chapter 10) that, in the end, generate competitive advantages such as customer delight, growth, and profitability by

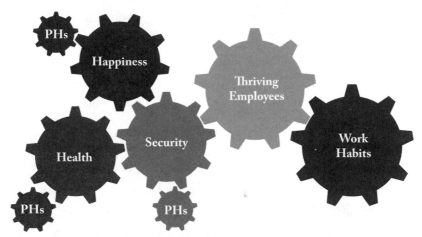

Figure 3.3: The Machinery of High-Performance Employers

improving strategy, execution, product development, management, innovation, and a range of other high-order success drivers.

High-performance employers succeed at making it easy for employees to practice these habits and can expect a more stable and lower-cost workforce as a result. The sustainability that emerges is why high-performance employers enjoy a lasting competitive advantage. Note that a significant reason why employees are happy (or not) at work is the way they are treated by their managers and peers. Management and the habits they practice are a critical driver of the engagement of employees, as they have an outsized impact on employee happiness and fulfillment.

Now that we've made the case for pivotal habits as a key driver of the performance of your business, we can ask how we design the workplace to make these habits easier for employees to practice.

References

Burgomaster, K. A., Howarth, K. R., Phillips, S. M., Rakobowchuk, M., MacDonald, M. J., McGee, S. L., & Gibala, M. J. (2008). Similar metabolic adaptations during exercise after low volume sprint interval and traditional endurance training in humans. *Journal of Physiology*, *586*, 151–160. doi:10.1113/jphysiol.2007.142109

Cappuccio, F. P., Taggart, F. M., Kandala, N. B., Currie, A., Peile, E., Stranges, S., & Miller, M. A. (2008). Meta-analysis of short sleep duration and obesity in children and adults. Sleep, *31*(5), 619–626.

Cauter, E. V., Knutson, K., Leproult, R., & Spiegel, K. (2005). The impact of sleep deprivation on hormones and metabolism. Medscape. Retrieved from https://www.medscape.org/viewarticle/502825

Ciccolo, J. T., Dunsiger, S. I., Williams, D. M., Bartholomew, J. B., Jennings, E. G., Ussher, M. H., Kraemer, W. J., & Marcus, B. H. (2011). Resistance training as an aid to standard smoking cessation treatment: a pilot study. *Nicotine and Tobacco Research*, *13*(8), 756–760.

Cochran, A. J., Percival, M. E., Tricarico, S., Little, J. P., Cermak, N., Gillen, J. B., Tarnopolsky, M. A., & Gibala, M. J. (2014). Intermittent and continuous high-intensity exercise training induce similar acute but different chronic muscle adaptations. *Experimental Physiology*, *99*, 782–791. doi:10.1113/expphysiol.2013.077453

Como, M. (2011). Do happier people make more money? An empirical study of the effect of a person's happiness on their income. *Park Place Economist, 19*. Retrieved from http://digitalcommons.iwu.edu/parkplace/vol19/iss1/8

Dimeo, F. D., Pagonas, N., Seibert, F., Arndt, R., Zidek, W., & Westhoff, T. H. (2012). Aerobic exercise reduces blood pressure in resistant hypertension. *Hypertension*, *60*, 653–658.

Drummond, S. P. A., Paulus, M. P., & Tapert, S. F. (2006). Effects of two nights sleep deprivation and two nights recovery sleep on response inhibition. *Journal of Sleep Research*, *15*(3), 261–265. doi:10.1111/j.1365-2869.2006.00535.x

Dum, R. P., Levinthal, D. J., & Strick P. L. (2016). Motor, cognitive, and affective areas of the cerebral cortex influence the adrenal medulla.

Proceedings of the National Academy of Sciences, 113(35), 9922–9927. doi:10.1073/pnas.1605044113

Egerton, T., Chastin, S. F. M., Stensvold, D., & Helbostad, J. L. (2017). Fatigue may contribute to reduced physical activity among older people: An observational study. *Journal of Gerontology A, 71*(5), 670–676. doi:10.1093/gerona/glv15

Ewert, B. (2016). Phone interview with Dawn Reiss.

Frederickson, B. (2004). The broaden-and-build theory of positive emotions. *Philosophical Transactions of the Royal Society of London B, 359*, 1367–1377.

Garman, E. T. (2004). The importance of workplace financial education to employers. American Express Guide to Workplace Financial Education and Advice. Indianapolis: Wellness Council of Indiana. Retrieved from http://www.wellnessindiana.org/wp-content/uploads/2012/07/Employee-Financial-Stress-is-Costing-Your-Company-a-Bundle.pdf

Garman, V. E. T., Leech, I. E., & Grable, J. E. (1996). The negative impact of employee poor personal financial. *Financial Counseling and Planning, 7*, 157–168.

Garoarsdóttir, R. B., & Dittmar, H. (2012). The relationship of materialism to debt and financial well-being: The case of Iceland's perceived prosperity. *Journal of Economic Psychology, 33*(3), 471.

Gillen, J. B., Martin, B. J., MacInnis, M. J., Skelly, L. E., Tarnopolsky, M. A., & Gibala, M. J. (2016). Twelve weeks of sprint interval training improves indices of cardiometabolic health similar to traditional endurance training despite a five-fold lower exercise volume and time commitment. *PLoS ONE, 11*(4), e0154075. doi:10.1371/journal.pone.0154075

Hagberg, J. M., Park, J., & Brown, M. D. (2000). The role of exercise training in the treatment of hypertension: An update. *Sports Medicine, 30*(3), 193–206.

Harrison, Y., & Horne, J. A. (1999). One night of sleep loss impairs innovative thinking and flexible decision making. *Organizational Behavior and Human Decision Processes, 78*(2), 128–145. doi:10.1006/obhd.1999.2827

Herzog, S. (2016). Phone interview with Dawn Reiss.

Hogenkamp, P. S., Nilsson, E., Nilsson, V. C., Chapman, C. D., Vogel, H., Lundberg, L. S., Zarei, S., Cedermaes, J., Rangtell, F. H., Broman, J., Dickson, S. L., Brunstrom, J. M., Benedict, C., & Schioth, H. B. (2013). Acute sleep deprivation increases portion size and affects food choice in young men. *Psychoneuroendocrinology, 38*(9), 1668–1674.

Horne, J. A. (1988). Sleep loss and "divergent" thinking ability. *Sleep, 11*(6), 528–536.

Joo, S.-H. (1998). Personal financial wellness and worker job productivity. Doctoral dissertation. Retrieved from https://vtechworks.lib.vt.edu/handle/10919/30519?show=full

Kim, I., Park, S., Chou, T., Trombold, J. R., & Coyle, E. F. (2016). Prolonged sitting negatively affects the postprandial plasma triglyceride-lowering effect of acute exercise. *American Journal of Physiology: Endocrinology and Metabolism, 311*(5), E891–E898.

King, A. C., Oman, R. F., Brassinton, G. S., Bliwise, D. L., & Haskell, W. L. (1997). Moderate-intensity exercise and self-rated quality of sleep in older adults. *JAMA, 227*, 32–37.

Landrigan, C. P., Rothschild, J. M., Cronin, J. W., Kaushal, R., Burdick, E., Katz, J. T., et al. (2004). Effect of reducing interns' work hours on serious medical errors in intensive care units. *New England Journal of Medicine, 351*(18), 1838–1848.

Lee, D., Artero, E. G., Sui, X., & Blair, S. N. (2010). Mortality trends in the general population: The importance of cardiorespiratory fitness. *Journal of Psychopharmacology, 24* Suppl 27–35. doi:10.1177/1359786810382057

McKenna, F. P., Warburton, D. M., & Winwood, M. (1993). Exploring the limits of optimism: The smoker's decision making. *British Journal of Psychology, 84,* 389–394.

Moholdt, T. T., Amundsen, H., Rustad, B. H., Wahba, L. A., Løvø, A., Gullikstad, K. T., Bye, L. R., Skogvoll, E., Wisløff, U. & Slørdahl, S. A. (2009). Aerobic interval training versus continuous moderate exercise after coronary artery bypass surgery: A randomized study of cardiovascular effects and quality of life. *American Heart Journal, 158,* 1031–1037.

Pinetti, S. (2016). Personal interview with Hanlie van Wyk.

PricewaterhouseCoopers (PWC). (2011). Financial Wellness Survey. Retrieved from http://www.pwc.com/us/en/pressreleases/2011/cash-and-debt-management-issues.jhtml

Puetz, T. W., O'Connor, P. J., & Dishman, R. K. (2006). Effects of chronic exercise on feelings of energy and fatigue: A quantitative synthesis. *Psychological Bulletin, 132*(6), 866–876.

Reid, K. J., Baron, K. G., Lu, B., Naylor, E., Wolfe, L., & Zee, P. C. (2010). Aerobic exercise improves self-reported sleep and quality of life in older adults with insomnia. *Sleep Medicine, 11*(9), 934–940. doi:10.1016/j.sleep.2010.04.014

Revell, A. D. (1988). Smoking and performance—a puff-by-puff analysis. *Psychopharmacology, 96*(4), 563–565.

Rivett, J. (2016). Phone interview with Dawn Reiss.

Robertson, I., & Cooper. G. (2011). *Well-being: Productivity and happiness at work.* Cham, Switzerland: Palgrave McMillan.

Shepell·fgi Research Group. (2009). Financial Distress Impacts Health and Productivity: Employees Turning to EAP for Help Insights from the Shepell·fgi Research Group. Toronto, Ontario, Canada: Shepell·fgi Research Group.

Smith, B. (2016). Phone interview with Dawn Reiss.

Sui, X., Lee, D., Matthews, C. E., Adams, S. A., Hébert, J. R., Church, T. S., Lee, C. D., & Blair, S. N. (2010). The influence of cardiorespiratory fitness on lung cancer mortality. *Medicine and Science in Sports and Exercise, 42*(5), 872–878. doi:10.1249/MSS.0b013e3181c47b65

Tjønna, A. E., Lee, S. J., Rognmo, O., Stolen, T. O., Bye, A., et al. (2008). Aerobic interval training versus continuous moderate exercise as a treatment for the metabolic syndrome: A pilot study. *Circulation, 118*, 346–354.

Tjønna, A. E., Leinan, I. M., Thoresen Bartnes, A., Jenssen, B. M., Gibala, M. J., Winett, R. A., & Wisløff, U. (2013). Low- and high-volume of intensive endurance training significantly improves maximal oxygen uptake after 10 weeks of training in healthy men. *PLoS ONE, 8*(5), e65382.

White, D., Goldsmith, K., Johnson, A. L., Chalder, T., Sharpe, M., & the PACE Trial Management Group. (2013). Recovery from chronic fatigue syndrome after treatments given in the PACE trial. *Psychological Medicine, 43*, 2227–2235.

Youngstedt, S. D. (2005). Effects of exercise on sleep. *Clinics in Sports Medicine, 24*(2), 355-365. doi:10.1016/j.csm.2004.12.003

Zelenski, J. M., Murphy, S. A. & Jenkins, D. A. (2008). The happy-productive worker thesis revisited. *Journal of Happiness Studies, 9*, 521–537.

Zhang, P., Sui, X., Hand, G. A., Hébert, J. R., & Blair, S. N. (2014). Association of changes infitness and body composition with cancer mortality in men. *Medicine and Science in Sports and Exercise, 46*(7), 1366–1374. doi:10.1249/MSS.0000000000000225

4

The World of Context

When you're doing mountain rescue, you don't take a doctorate in mountain rescue; you look for somebody who knows the terrain. It's about context.

—Rory Stewart, diplomat, politician, and writer

Joan has been sitting at the casino slot machine for more than three hours. She's consistently losing money and is more than $500 in the hole. You've been watching her, wondering:

a) Why is she having such a good time, enthralled by the spin of the reels?
b) When will she decide enough is enough and stop throwing good money after bad?

Deep in the coding that runs the machine is an algorithm that determines how often and how much you win, on average. The pattern includes a much greater number of near misses than you'd randomly expect. Two sevens followed by a cherry. Two cherries followed by a lemon. Joan's heart rate rises, she holds her breath, she experiences a frisson of excitement—only to become disappointed with the next near miss yet anxious to bet again. She feels she's on the verge of the BIG win, so she's determined to stay at this "hot machine" just a little longer, pumping more and more money into it.

Game designers know that the compulsion to stay and gamble more is stimulated by the near miss even more so than by a win. Dopamine is released into our brains in response to uncertainty in our environment, whether in the form of a threat or a reward. As one seven comes up and then the second, you believe you are a moment away from either a sensational win or a small consolation prize, and your body is flooded with anticipation. Even when you lose, the dopamine continues to surge through your brain, and you are still "on the hunt."

Gambling is for adults what opening Christmas presents is for kids. It drives the same insatiable desire for more, regardless of the wins or losses. If we judge Joan as weak-willed, our focus is on the wrong thing. We don't see and appreciate the many ways in which the game (and her surroundings) have been carefully designed to create an experience and an environment that make it very difficult for her to leave until her last cent is spent. To truly understand her behavior, we have to evaluate everything that surrounds her. It's not just the near misses that compel her to stay but also the way a casino is designed, the loud noises and sirens that blare when someone wins, the low lighting and absence of natural light to ensure we lose track of time, and the free drinks that are often served to big gamblers to ensure they are happy, uninhibited, and inclined to take more risks. Of course, we convince ourselves that if we were in the same situation, we would behave differently. But would we? It's the entire context of the gambling experience that has such a mesmerizing influence on Joan and millions of others who love nothing more than a trip to Vegas.

Now let me give you an everyday example of the power of context. Next time you enter a grocery store, notice which direction you automatically take. If you live in the US, chances are you enter the store, immediately turn right, and move in an counterclockwise direction. We carry the familiar rules of the road with us into the grocery store and use the same rules when walking on the sidewalk. If you live in the UK, your pattern would be the reverse of that in the US. This often leads to the comical outcome of visitors from the UK bumping into other pedestrians when in the US and vice versa.

It's not just rules that influence us but also the people who surround us and the way they behave. Look at the picture below. Compare the left line with the three lines on the right: A, B, and C. Which of these three lines is the same length as the line on the left?

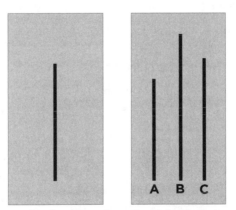

Figure 4.1: From the Asch conformity experiments

The obvious answer is C. But in a famous experiment, conducted by psychologist Solomon Asch, numerous people gave an incorrect answer—because they were swayed by other participants who had been coached to deliberately and convincingly give the wrong answer. In 12 separate trials, on average, one-third of the people were "persuaded" to answer incorrectly at least once. The social pressure from the co-conspirators overwhelmed them.

Sometimes the "others" don't even have to be present in the flesh. As social media becomes pervasive, the other people can be our Facebook friends who post overly positive representations of their lives. It's one of the explanations for so-called Facebook-induced depression. When we compare our mundane lives to the apparently rah-rah lifestyle of our friends (nothing but good times, parties, and celebrations), it can make us envious and depressed.

The common thread in these scenarios—the casino, the supermarket, and the social world—is that we behave in response to influences from outside of ourselves. It could be the physical environment (lights, noises, and the design of the space), a rule we are used to following (driving on the right-hand side of the road), or people who influence us (the co-conspirators in that length of the line experiment).

An Error of Focus

One of the reasons we don't notice the influence of all of these environmental features is because we are so focused on ourselves and on other people when we think about changing behavior. We have an engineering mind-set that seeks to find a problem, diagnose it, and then fix it. It's a completely appropriate mind-set for many problems, but in the case of human behavior, if we focus on the people, we are likely to conclude that they are the problem—that they're either not smart enough, not motivated enough, lack willpower, don't have common sense, or exhibit some other human failing.

We conclude that the individual needs fixing, and we fail to appreciate the enveloping environment. Physicians, health insurance designers, benefits managers, financial fitness instructors, and happiness gurus often insist, "We could really help if people would just do X." Implicit in that statement is the assumption that it is the person who is largely to blame, and, therefore, the solution is to fix the person. This approach totally misses what really explains much of people's behavior: the contexts in which we live our lives.

What Is a Life Context?

So what exactly do we mean by a life context? Think about a fish swimming in the sea. The water is the context for that fish's life and completely influences how the fish moves, breathes, eats, and reproduces. The water defines every aspect of the fish's life. Yet the fish probably doesn't notice the water itself, just like we don't notice the air that we breathe until it's highly polluted or no longer there.

If you want the fish to behave differently, you could lure it with food, or you could introduce a current into the water (the kind that moves the water in one direction, not the electrical kind, although that too would undoubtedly change the fish's behavior). You could also heat or cool the water to encourage the fish to swim in a particular direction. Managing the water is the best way to manage the fish's behavior without making it feel too uncomfortable.

For our purposes, there are three properties of the water that are interesting:

1. The water is all encompassing and completely surrounds the fish at all times. The water is the background inside of which the life of the fish plays out.
2. The water influences every aspect of the fish's life.
3. The fish almost certainly does not notice that influence, even though the water is the context for its entire life.

Similarly, human beings live inside of contexts that are (1) in the background and (2) strongly influence our actions, yet (3) we don't often notice them.

1. A life context constantly "surrounds" us, even though it might be "in the background." Regard a context as a stage on which life plays out. When you go to see a theatrical performance, the stage set has a dramatic impact on how you interpret and enjoy the play, even though your focus is primarily on the actors themselves. The stage completely surrounds the actors and is the context for the lives of the characters being portrayed.

2. A life context highly influences how we behave. Extending the metaphor of the stage, the position of the various props (furniture, staircases, curtains, lights) has a considerable influence on how the actors play their parts. It would make little sense if Romeo were serenading Juliet and she wasn't on the balcony but standing behind him on the stage! In the same way, our life contexts highly influence the ways we think and act.

3. A life context, despite its influence, generally goes unnoticed at the conscious level despite its influence. We mostly focus on something that's happening right in front of our eyes and fail to appreciate the wider picture of our environment.

When you appreciate life contexts, you can design methods of influence into them and help to cultivate the behavior and habits you desire in yourself and others. Designing contexts in a way that makes it easy for us to create new habits is critically important in creating human habits. However, one of the reasons why creating new habits in others and ourselves is so difficult is because there are **four** distinct contexts to think about, to understand, and to design.

The Four Contexts

The Four Contexts that surround us are:

- The Systems Context
- The Spaces Context
- The Social Context
- The Context of the Self

Let's now define and understand each of these a little better.

The Systems Context

Systems include:

- Regulations, laws, and rules. For example, countries have a law about which side of the road to drive on. Rules can be enshrined in law but can sometimes just be societal agreements. Laws regarding firearm ownership differ in Japan and the US and most likely explain a large part of the massive difference in gun-related deaths and accidents in the two countries.
- Customs. We shake hands when we meet people in America, but we bow when we meet someone in Japan.
- Mental shortcuts or heuristics. These help us make decisions or judgments quickly, on the basis of limited information. They are systems because they follow a process or formula.
- Business processes. These are the "recipes" that we follow to complete complex tasks, such as assembling a car or writing a business proposal.
- Business policies. For example, these can be policies on vacation time, dress code, or working hours.

- Language. Language can be considered a system, because rules such as grammar and vocabulary are constraints on how we think and the ideas we can express.
- Design rules. In the early days of the World Wide Web, as an example, website designs all followed a similar set of rules, displaying specific tabs across the top of a page. These design rules encoded in these websites, rather than the visual displays, trained many of us to navigate these sites in a certain way. To this day, most of us expect to see an "about us" tab somewhere at the top of a business website.

Systems are almost by definition abstract and expressed in language of one form or another (three examples: English, the coding language C++, or the language of formal logic). They are not physically tangible, but their influence is pervasive.

The Spaces Context

Spaces are made up of the physical environment in which we live. We see most aspects of them, but not all. Others are sensed using our noses, ears, or other sense organs. The walls, ceiling, floors, furniture, and corridors that make up our work space affect the way we sit, stand, or move. Physical spaces also include:

- Elements of design and architecture, including the height of standard desks and ceilings, the placement of doors, the slope of floors, and other elements that define our homes, workplaces, and public spaces.
- Light, shading, and light gradients. We are often guided through public spaces by how designers use light to create pathways.
- Odors and odor gradients. Retailers and hotels commonly have a scent logo or signature smell that permeates their

locations, helping to stimulate an unforgettable experience, because our sense of smell and memories are closely linked.

- Textures and colors. Food designers talk about mouthfeel and the ways in which crispness, crunchiness, chewiness, moistness, creaminess, crustiness, and other attributes affect not only how food feels but also how it tastes and how we judge whether we like it.
- Virtual worlds. For many of us, our time is increasingly spent "inside" computer screens and websites, reading office documents, participating in chat rooms, or gawking at social media sites. We experience the virtual world as if it's physical. Five to 15-year-olds spend up to 15 hours a week online, while even kids as young as three or four are engrossed online as much as eight hours a week. The next evolution of virtual reality will take the experience once step further, creating virtual spaces that we experience as literally being inside.

You might wonder how Spaces can be a context, because one of the defining elements of a context is that we don't notice it. The answer is that we don't notice the *influence* of a context, especially our physical spaces. It's called "environmental blindness." But it's also true that we often don't notice the spaces themselves and what's in them. Take a look in your boardroom. Odds are there are some cords lying in the corner, piles of paperwork, or some other kind of small mess. What might bother us initially (that chip in the kitchen sink) often becomes familiar and unnoticed relatively quickly. If you have teenagers and you've ever asked them to clean up the mess in their rooms, only to receive the response "What mess?" you've experienced environmental blindness firsthand!

The Social Context

The people with whom we interact are part of our environment and exert a much stronger influence over our lives than inanimate objects. After all, people are able to speak, move, make eye contact, point, and employ many other gestures that direct our behavior. The way we feel about other people, whether that feeling is love, hate, indifference, or irritation, often dictates the choices we make. We are influenced more or less depending on our view of people's occupation, education, status, age, gender, religion, and race.

Even if we are not being racist, sexist, or any other "-ist," we still notice and may be influenced by these characteristics. Social influence is strongly transmitted visually, as we watch each other for cues as to how to behave. Researchers have noticed how, over time, groups of interconnected people stopped smoking in concert, leaving smokers on the periphery of the social networks. Mirror neurons in our brains prime us to act in ways similar to how other people act. But we also choose to follow the actions of others to avoid embarrassment. Have you ever, for instance:

- Laughed at a joke you didn't get because everyone else was laughing?
- Gone to a party or event when you didn't really feel like it so your friends wouldn't call you a party pooper?
- Had another shot of tequila, or slice of cheesecake, because everyone else was doing so?
- Joined in the teasing of someone in your group, thankful that it wasn't directed at you?

Admitting to these behaviors is embarrassing, but very few people can honestly claim they've never done at least one of the things on that list.

When considering habits and the influence of other people, it's useful to make a comparison with infectious diseases (perhaps not a tasteful analogy but an instructive one). Disease spreads because a virus or bacteria is transmitted from one person to another via physical contact. The virus then reproduces, expands somewhere in the body, and wreaks havoc. For ideas to spread effectively, they should be expressed in a way that allows them to be seen, or spoken about, so that they can "infect" the next brain.

If you want to get people to act with consistency (or practice a habit), you have to first present the action as an idea. Then, you have to figure out how to make that idea highly contagious and, finally, how to imbue the idea with either the flexibility to mutate (running the risk that the original idea becomes obsolete) or the resilience to survive an onslaught of attacks from competitors with new ideas. Successfully designing the Social Context relies heavily on understanding how ideas spread from one human being to another and what makes them stick in our minds. For instance, what makes one advertising jingle an earworm and another one totally forgettable?

It's also important to note the kinds of people who have the most influence over us. In general, they are:

- People we see most often, which explains the endorsement power of those reality TV "stars" who are famous for being famous.
- People we like and trust or admire.
- People we think are similar to us.
- People we regard as superior to us in a way we respect.

Researchers have also identified two major instigators of opinion: (1) the expert effect and (2) the majority effect. The expert effect is induced by the presence of a highly confident (and perhaps credentialed) individual in a group, while the majority effect is caused by the presence of a critical mass of laypeople sharing similar opinions.

Systems, Spaces, and Social contexts are the three more obvious contexts. However, the final context, the Context of the Self, requires a little more thought to understand.

The Context of the Self

How can we be a context for our own lives? It doesn't seem to make sense at first. But we absolutely influence our own lives and actions, in ways we don't notice or can't even completely control. Let's start with the things we think—or rather the things we think we think! Have you ever really thought about who it is that's doing the thinking in your head? It certainly feels like we are the agents of those thoughts, and they are certainly happening IN our heads, so who else could be responsible? Well, if you are the actor in the thinking that goes on inside your head, then you should be able to choose NOT TO THINK. Try that for a few minutes and see how you do!

The reality is that thoughts are streaming through our consciousness all the time, and only with some difficulty do we control those thoughts. Mostly, thoughts are automatic, arriving in response to the things we see, smell, feel, taste, or sense; sometimes they pop up randomly. Consider the difference between actively thinking about how to solve a math problem versus sitting on the train on the way to work watching fellow commuters. In both situations, your mind is filled with a stream of thoughts, but in the latter case, they seem to just emerge into existence from nowhere.

We appear to have a voice in our heads that is perpetually commenting on life around us. First, it may judge how badly the person ahead of us is driving. Next, it may wonder whether we remembered to lock the door when we left home. Then, just as suddenly, we're smiling at the memory of spring break, prompted by a song that comes on the radio that was played nonstop the last spring break of your high school years. If you stop to listen to the voice and set it aside as if it were someone else, you might notice that it has a personality all its own.

For some, the voice in their head is a harsh critic (of other people, of themselves, or both). For others, that voice always seems to be shouting about the dangers and risks of a situation and warning us not to take action. In the best-case scenario, this voice is like an overprotective parent. In the worst case, it's like a tyrannical boss. Notice, too, that it doesn't seem to have very good manners. Our internal voice doesn't say, "I wonder whether the guy in front is driving erratically because he's suffering a heart attack and needs help." No. It says, "That jerk is a menace. Scream at him and honk the horn NOW!"

This stream of consciousness might appear to be harmless, but it does have an effect on how we feel and the things we do and choose not to do. These automatic and persistent thoughts, combined with the stories we actively tell ourselves, powerfully influence our actions. We make up stories about everything, from the smallest errors we make to the biggest events in our lives, and we use those stories to guide our actions. Many of those stories are old and have been playing in our heads for such a long time that we believe them to be true, even when they aren't.

Here's an example: Mark remembers when he was five years old and along with his four siblings was running around the kitchen, getting under his mom's feet. Recently widowed, she found it hard to cope and was often exhausted and exasperated. On this particular day, Mark ran into her, making her drop a hot plate of dinner over herself and over Mark's shoulder and face. Both were burned, but not too badly. In tears, Mark wanted nothing more than for his mother to hold him until he felt better. However, overcome by exhaustion and the shock of burning both of them, she lashed out, shouting,

"Sometimes I hate all of you." Instantly, she regretted her outburst, but the damage was done. In that moment, Mark made up a story about himself. It went something like: "I made my mom angry and cry. I seem to do that a lot. She says she doesn't love me. I must not be lovable." The story of "I'm not lovable" stuck. And it became the story that ruled his life.

Now picture Mark as an adult who considers himself unlovable and reflect on the ways he behaves. He enters romantic relationships expecting them to end (after all, who would stay around if they don't love you?). He invests little in other people, because there is no expectation of love in return. He's prone to sulk and feel bitter at the unfairness of a world where others find love and he does not. By Mark's fiftieth birthday, after three divorces and a string of failed relationships, he's estranged from his five children and feels utterly alone and lonely. It wasn't until his therapist helped him see how the five-year-old Mark was still running his life, influencing his decisions and making him act in certain ways. He could look back and trace all the misery to that moment 45 years earlier.

Of course, it is an oversimplification to say that we are the way we are as an adult because of one thing that happened as a child. Whether the source of our stories is something catastrophic or something as minor as a fifth-grade friend spitefully telling us that we have funny teeth, it can influence the way we live our lives for the rest of our lives. What makes this even sadder is that often the stories are just not true. We relate to our stories as if they are 100 percent true, but we are hopeless at separating what really happened from what we have imagined. For example, our fifth-grade friend might well have ridiculed our teeth, in retaliation for being called ugly—something we conveniently forgot. She was probably just lashing out, and there was no truth to her statement, but you could be stuck in its grasp for years, embarrassed to crack a smile in case people would see your bad teeth.

We are a walking library of stories about ourselves and other people that dictate how we live our lives. We are not, however, helpless against these negative stories. As we'll see, one of the best ways to assist people in adopting new habits is to help them recognize how their existing stories limit their abilities or help them invent new stories that empower them.

Let's recap. The Context of the Self is:

- The automatic and persistent thoughts streaming through our minds.
- The stories we have made up and carry with us about ourselves and others.
- The "facts" we have picked during our lives and the things we believe in, whether true or not.
- The opinions, generalizations, and prejudices we hold as a result.

The Self Context influences our actions because it acts as a filter through which new information is interpreted. As Anaïs Nin said, we don't see the world as it is; we see the world as we are!

The Context of the Self is vitally important to habit creation because the stories we tell ourselves can be:

- Barriers to taking action: "I don't earn enough money to be able to save for retirement."
- The source of a lack of confidence: "I'm just not the type of person who is ever going to be happy, so why even try meditation?"
- The source of motivation: "I have to lose weight and get in shape so I can find a loving relationship."
- The permission to succumb to temptation: "I have no willpower, so I am helpless to resist when offered chocolate."

Depending on the types of stories we tell ourselves, new habits can be either easier to create or damn near impossible.

Together, the four Contexts completely surround us, influencing how we think and act and, consequently, the results we get in life. If habits are our destiny, then context design is the solution to create whatever future we want for our companies and ourselves.

References

Asch, S. E. (1951). Effects of group pressure upon the modification and distortion of judgment. In H. Guetzkow (ed.) Groups, leadership and men. Pittsburgh, PA: Carnegie Press.

Andrews, S., Ellis, D. A., Shaw, H., & Piwek, L. (2015). Beyond self-report: Tools to compare estimated and real-world smartphone use. *PLoS ONE, 10*(10), e0139004. doi:10.1371/journal.pone.0139004

Eadicicco, L. (2015). Americans check their phones 8 billion times a day. *Time*. Retrieved from http://time.com/4147614/smartphone-usage-us-2015/

Gregoire, C. (2015). You probably use your smartphone way more than you think. HuffPost UK. Retrieved from http://www.huffingtonpost.com/entry/smartphone-usage-estimates_us_5637687de4b063179912dc96

Nelson, P. (2016). We touch our phones 2,617 times a day, says study. Networkworld. Retrieved from https://www.networkworld.com/article/3092446/smartphones/we-touch-our-phones-2617-times-a-day-says-study.html

5

The Four Powers

*The power for creating a better future
is contained in the present moment:
You create a good future by creating
a good present.*

—Eckhart Tolle

I t's hard for most people to adopt new habits. A lifetime of doing something one way doesn't change with the wave of a magic wand. Entrenched habits—good and bad—become a rigid part of who you are as a person. Habits make the man.

We've talked to thousands of people in the course of our research, some struggling to make better choices with their lives, others extremely successful in one domain but a hot mess in another. Insights we've gained from these conversations have been combined with our research on the science of behavior to create a model of how habits are formed. All in all, we've based our model and influence methods on a combination of academic research, best practices, and tested methods across multiple industries.

The conclusion of all this work is that there are four forces that act on us and make it easier or harder to create or change habits. These four forces are:

1. Capability—the sum of our confidence and competence
2. Motivation—our compulsion to act on our plans
3. Barriers—static impediments to making the changes we want
4. Temptations—active distractions from our best-laid plans

Together, they act on us, pushing or pulling us toward or away from certain actions. Barriers and Temptations are negative forces, generally preventing us from taking the actions we say we want to take. Capability and Motivation are positive forces, helping us to start, improve at, and become masters of any given habit. Think of this as a tug-of-war between the positive and negative forces. As the forces on one side increase, so the point of equilibrium moves, allowing a change of habits.

For each individual, one or more of these four forces may be more important or more impactful in a specific situation. For example, even if we are motivated to jog (as a form of exercise) and we are free of temptations (to stay in bed instead) and capable of doing so (not injured and confident we can succeed), we might be stopped by a barrier (such as extreme weather conditions or a neighborhood that is not safe enough to go for a run). For someone else, what might be lacking is the motivation to get up in the morning, despite having no barriers, temptations, or a lack of capability.

Capability and Motivation work together; one can sometimes make up for a lack in the other. If we are highly motivated to do something, we might persist even despite low initial capability. Think how focused you would be to learn to swim in order to prevent a child from drowning if he or she fell into a swimming pool. Similarly, if you are already highly capable at something, making a new related task relatively easy, you might not need much motivation to act. Of course, a complete lack of either Capability or Motivation will either ensure failure or prevent you from making an attempt in the first place.

Barriers and Temptations are often also simultaneously at play but less so in the way of making up for each other. For example, if you were considering putting money into a 401(k) plan, a relatively small barrier (I forgot my password for the enrollment system), combined with a relatively small temptation (and instead I could spend the money getting that new iPhone I really want), can add up to a potent combined force preventing you from taking the right action. Unlike Capability and Motivation, where a complete lack of one or the other ensures failure or inaction, a complete lack of either a Barrier or a Temptation does not ensure success. But it does make it more likely.

The goal is to make it easier for people to take action and create habits by removing or reducing Barriers and helping them to avoid or resist Temptations.

However, before we can start to design our world (our contexts) to make new habits easy, let's explain in more detail what we mean by the forces of Capability, Motivation, Barriers, and Temptations.

Capability, the Sum of Confidence and Competence

If I have the belief that I can do it, I shall surely acquire the capacity to do it even if I may not have it at the beginning.
—MAHATMA GANDHI

When motivation, desire, and even compulsion are high and no barriers or temptations are present, a lack of capability can still explain people's inability to act toward their stated goals. That's because capability is the sum of competence and confidence, and both are important when explaining why and how people act.

When lacking competence, people might say:

- "I didn't know how."
- "I didn't know where to start."
- "I wasn't sure of the best way."

When feeling a loss of confidence, they might say:

- "I'd lost faith that I could."
- "I'm not the kind of person who can . . ."
- "I don't have what it takes to . . ."
- "I've tried and failed many times before, so it's pointless."
- "I was scared of being embarrassed if I got it wrong."

Although confidence and competence are separate traits, they often grow together, one feeding the other. Without confidence, we're unlikely to take the first step. Without competence, we're likely to fail repeatedly and give up hope or lose confidence. It can be a vicious cycle.

Let's understand each one separately.

Competence: Competence involves having gained some level of mastery at a particular act, and it differs from mere ability. Here's an example. At age 15, most people are able to learn to drive even though they have not yet been able do so. By age 30, that potential ability has usually become a set of acquired skills and mental short-cuts, perhaps encoded in new brain wiring and muscle memory. We have become competent drivers. In fact, one of the ways we know we have become competent is whether we are able to complete tasks automatically or almost so. You've probably had the experience of not remembering your actual drive to work because your mind was otherwise engaged. You performed all the actions required to drive without even thinking about it.

Competence comes with repetition and is honed by failure, feedback, and progress. You achieve mastery when you have invested considerable time and effort into the deliberate practice of a given task. "Deliberate practice," a term coined by Swedish psychologist Anders Ericsson, an internationally recognized researcher in the psychological nature of expertise and human performance, is a route we seldom take, however. Instead, we mostly practice things repetitively. Think about learning to throw a basketball through a hoop. Repetitive practice involves throwing the ball at or through the hoop over and over again and noticing when it went through and when it missed. That feedback on hits or misses is useful and can guide us to improve, although the process is somewhat unconscious and, well, hit or miss. Importantly, improvement using only repetitive practice takes a long time and tends to level off at merely satisfactory performance.

Deliberate practice, on the other hand, involves a "mini-autopsy" after each throw. We pause and consider what we did, how we stood, and where we released the ball. Professionals may even review video evidence to seek clues as to what worked and what could be improved. What distinguishes deliberate practice from repetitive practice is the quantity of feedback considered, as well as the intentionality behind taking that feedback into account. The nature of the feedback is also different. In deliberate practice, we tend to focus on HOW we acted, in relation to the result we got, whereas in repetitive practice, we just look at the result itself. Although it seems like a slower process, the improvement in competence that comes from deliberate rather than repetitive practice is much greater. In summary: competence is the sum of applied knowledge turned into skills and improved through deliberate practice.

Confidence: Confidence is the strength of belief in one's own ability or power to act or succeed. Albert Bandura, widely described as one of the most influential psychologists of all time, has demonstrated how self-confidence, which is part of self-efficacy, affects how we approach a specific task, or even if we do so in the first instance.

A related concept is Rotter's locus of control, which refers to an individual's belief about where control over events resides: in simple terms, who or what is responsible for what happens to us. People with an *internal* locus of control believe that the power to change the world lives within them. People with an *external* locus of control believe that the world happens to them. As George Bernard Shaw famously said: "Reasonable people adapt themselves to the world. Unreasonable people attempt to adapt the world to themselves. All progress, therefore, depends on unreasonable people!"

As young children, we are quite fearless and willing to try almost anything. We don't lose confidence when we try something new and fail. We simply don't know any better! Pretty soon, we are at it again, exploring the world and constantly learning. At some point, though, we start to tell ourselves stories about who we are and what we are capable of doing, which colors our thinking about the things we should try to do. Ask a class of first-graders who can sing, and every hand in the class goes up. Ask a group of adults, and one or two shy hands may be raised. Everyone else has told themselves a story that they can't sing, based on an experience, perhaps something as trivial as being teased years earlier by a sibling who heard us singing in the shower. The question was not who can sing *well*, but who can sing *at all*. The answer is that practically everyone can sing, but our stories have shut down or diminished our confidence, and that stops us from acting or even thinking we can act, in this case to sing.

If you have decided you can't sing, you won't ever try karaoke, sing happy birthday (loudly), participate in Christmas carols, or even serenade yourself in the shower, in case someone hears you. None of this should materially affect your quality of life, but you have to recognize that it's you and the story you've created that lead to a future in which singing is absent. Similar negative stories or beliefs could be much more significant in your life or the lives of others. Consider these notorious stories:

- "Girls are not good at math and science" and the resulting low rates of girls studying certain science degrees, especially in male-dominated societies.
- "Black men are more prone to violence," a false narrative that often results in the erroneous and extreme use of violence against young black men, potentially resulting in retaliatory actions on their part.
- "Women should not run businesses," a chauvinist story that, at least in part, explains the tiny percentage of female CEOs and board directors.

It's the reasons we give ourselves that often define our ability, the stories we tell ourselves about what we can and cannot achieve in the world, the stories that only loosely correlate with our actual ability as human beings. Prior failures are one of the key ways that we lose confidence. Making up your own stories as you age is one thing, but being told these stories by adults when you are a child makes breaking free from their hold even more difficult. How do we overcome such stories? We'll explore the many ways later, but, briefly, there are three key methods by which we gain confidence in the face of disempowering beliefs:

1. By trial and error (and by small successes in some of those trials). Generally, the more we try, failing sometimes and

succeeding other times, the more confidence and competence we gain.

2. By watching other people succeed. We not only learn this
   way but also judge our competence based on seeing others
   perform well at something, especially if we consider ourselves just as capable.
3. By mental practice. Imagining ourselves succeeding and
   mentally practicing the steps to get there build confidence.

Without the confidence to start, competence never builds. As
competence builds, confidence increases, which is why these two
traits are combined into the idea of capability. Although both sides
of this same coin are important, perhaps the most ignored area of
focus in habit creation solutions is addressing the lack of confidence
in the people we are trying to help. As such, it is often the biggest
opportunity to make a difference.

Motivation

The most difficult thing is the decision to act, the rest is mere tenacity."
—AMELIA EARHART

For many, the issue of motivation lies in how they describe their
inability to act. They may say things like:

- "I just didn't feel like it."
- "I ran out of willpower."
- "I wasn't motivated enough."
- "I guess I just don't want it enough."

This self-talk points to a fundamental misunderstanding about
desire, motivation, and compulsions. The *Oxford* dictionary definition

of motivation is the "desire or willingness to do something." And many of us think that one of the reasons we don't succeed at creating new habits is because we just don't have enough of this property. We have a slightly different view. Ask yourself the following questions (or test them with a group). First, "Do I really want to be healthy, or happy, or financially secure?" You are likely to find that the answer is a resounding "yes." Second, "How well is that working out for me?" The answer might be, in all likelihood, "Not so well." For most people, this thought experiment reveals two truths: one, that they *already* have a strong desire for many things in their lives and, two, that mere desire on its own is not enough to ensure that these things are achieved.

Of course, there are many stories about people single-mindedly going after a goal they really want and often succeeding against all odds. The appeal of these stories is that they give us hope, since this is not how it usually goes in real life. If merely wanting something is not enough, what is? While the feeling of desire can orient us toward an action, the kind of motivation that really works is more like a compulsion. It is an **irresistible** urge to behave in a certain way, even against one's conscious wishes. We desire to save for retirement but feel compelled to upgrade to the newest iPhone!

Wouldn't life be easier if we could figure out a way to be compelled to act on the things we know are really good for us? To do that, we must understand the difference between mere desire and compulsion at a deeper level. Part of the answer lies in neurochemistry. In the 1990s, researchers regarded serotonin and dopamine as the two pleasure hormones, flooding our brains in response to receiving a reward and leaving us feeling good. Subsequent research on dopamine revealed that its role is quite different. Dopamine is less about pleasure and reward and more about drive and survival, according to Nora Volkow, a neuroscientist and director of the National Institute on

Drug Abuse. One function of dopamine is to prepare us to act, rather than to reward us when that action generates a pleasurable result.

Dopamine helps to prepare the mind and body for action and ensures that we pay attention to the action that needs to be taken. Watch children preparing to open Christmas presents and you see the triumph of dopamine over serotonin and of compulsion over desire. Even when a child discovers that Santa has delivered exactly what he or she wanted, the unknown of what's inside the other gifts ensures a release of dopamine that drives him or her onward to tear open the wrapping on each present until every last one is opened. And it still leaves the child wanting more.

Dismayed parents, who put so much effort into buying and wrapping the gifts, can take comfort in the fact that their kids are in the grip of a dopamine rush that's equivalent to an adult's cocaine or gambling addiction. Forcing kids to fully appreciate each gift, one at a time, feels the same to the child's brain as being forced to hold your breath underwater—not a pleasant feeling at all. The key to being motivated enough or compelled to do the things we want to do is discovering how to release dopamine in our brains. Once you understand that it is not the reward itself that's the key motivating agent but the release of dopamine by our brains, you have the keys to unlock success.

Let's look at this in a business context. The standard approach to driving better performance is to offer incentives such as commission on sales, performance bonuses, or an increase in hourly pay. Traditional economic theory says that the greater the reward is, the stronger the motivation to act will be. But this does not match what we now know about the role of dopamine: rather, the better a reward is at releasing dopamine in our brains, the better it is at compelling action. The *value* of a reward and its dopamine-releasing potential are generally not very well correlated.

At the extremes, a reward of $1 million may compel people to participate in reality TV challenges such as eating putrid meat or surviving in a chamber of mosquitoes for 10 minutes. But social media and gaming companies have figured out that you can compel people to act much more cheaply, even at a cost close to zero. Next time you pick up your mobile phone to check whether you have a message, realize that you are responding to the release of dopamine in your brain. There is a surprise in not knowing whether we have a new message, and that ensures that our brains are primed, by dopamine, to pay attention. It is the reason we keep picking up our phones, to check, again and again.

Because dopamine release happens so quickly and is reabsorbed quickly, the compulsion to act can appear and disappear just as quickly. As we have come to understand the role of dopamine more clearly, it has become apparent that saying that you want something, or even feeling the desire for something, is a chasm away from being compelled to act. And the type of motivation that we need to create new habits is this compulsion, rather than mere desire.

Barriers

. . . human beings place upon an object, or a person, this responsibility of being the obstacle when the obstacle lies always within one's self.
—**ANAÏS NIN,** *THE DIARY OF ANAÏS NIN*

To understand the many barriers that people face, or think they face, we ask: "What got in the way of your creating or changing a habit?" The most common answers we hear are:

- "I didn't have enough time."
- "I didn't have enough money."

- "I forgot."
- "I didn't get the opportunity to . . ."
- "I didn't have permission to . . ."

No matter how they phrase their reasons, people generally point to a lack of time, money, opportunity, or permission. These barriers are static, as they don't change much over time. Take the distance between your home and your gym, for example. The distance never changes, but on the days you just don't feel like exercising, it might feel too far.

Some of the barriers are nothing more than excuses. "I didn't have time to go to the gym" is a classic example. We all share the same 24 hours in each day, and many people find the time to work out. What we're really saying is "I had other things that I prioritized above going to the gym." Of course, it's much easier to recognize this excuse-making in others than it is in ourselves. It can be infuriating when someone offers up the "no time to exercise" excuse, especially if he or she is brazen enough to do so while watching TV. On the other hand, you may not feel quite the same way when your favorite program is being aired. Just because some barriers are "made up" doesn't mean they're not powerful in stopping us from changing our habits. In fact, perhaps the made-up barriers and excuses are all the more powerful because we made them up!

Temptations

Arthur Dent: What happens if I press this button?
Ford Prefect: I wouldn't.
Arthur Dent: Oh.
Ford Prefect: What happened?
Arthur Dent: A sign lit up, saying, 'Please do not press this button again.'
—DouGLAS ADAMS,
THE ORIGINAL HITCHHIKER RADIO SCRIPTS

Temptations, like barriers, get in the way of planned action. Unlike barriers, which are largely static, temptations are often dynamic. As our behavior starts to change, so the forces of temptation increase, trying to pull us back into our old habits. In a way, they "fight back" when we start to get good at dealing with them because of the two sources of temptations: other people and companies.

People as the source of temptation: There's always someone ready to lead you astray. A person who, accidentally or deliberately (for his or her own motives), sabotages your efforts to create good habits. Smokers trying to quit the habit inevitably encounter friends or colleagues encouraging them to "just have one." Friends can also tempt us away from good habits such as exercise by suggesting that we go out for drinks or dinner instead. Family members can entice us away from good financial choices by putting forward a case for some splendid extravagance. Similarly, when you go to lunch with a group of people, it takes only one person to choose to have dessert to erode everybody else's willpower.

In part, such socially contagious habits (such as ordering cheese-cake) are explained by mirror neurons in our brains. These are neurons that lie next to motor neurons (the nerve cells that control mainly muscles and glands) that fire in response to the actions of other people and prime us to take similar actions. They explain why we tend to yawn when we see other people yawn or even when we hear or read the word "yawn," as you may be doing right now! The survival advantage of these mirror neurons is that they are likely to have primed our ancestors to take actions similar to those that they saw in others. If someone in your tribe suddenly jumps up and runs away, isn't it smart to do the same, rather than wait to see for yourself the saber-toothed tiger charging around the corner? Mirror neurons prepare the relevant muscles for action even before we are aware of the necessity to act.

In their book *Connected*, Nicholas Christakis and James Fowler analyzed data from the Framingham Heart Study and showed a correlation between people's health habits and health status and those of people with whom they were connected. On the positive side, they found that we are about 25 percent more likely to be happy if connected to a happy person. On the negative side, we are about 57 percent more likely to gain weight if a friend gains weight, especially a friend of the same gender. Worst of all, the percentage goes even higher when our spouse gains weight.

And it is not just our friends that influence us. The actions or habits of people we don't even know, connected to us by friends and friends of friends, can impact our lives. It's an effect that seems to occur up to three degrees of separation from ourselves. The habits of people you don't know can be affecting your own life right now. Other studies have shown that exercising, starting and quitting tobacco, losing and gaining weight, productivity at work, loneliness, and even suicide are socially contagious phenomena.

Companies as the source of temptation: There's an army of marketers, advertising experts, consumer behaviorists, and retail designers working tirelessly to encourage us to buy products or to fund their charities. They strive to turn us into lifetime customers or supporters, even fanatics "addicted" to their offerings.

A notable example that's been exposed over the years is big tobacco, whose cunning marketing and sales tactics have been curtailed and even banned in some countries. As compensation for the devastating health impact they have wrought, tobacco manufacturers have been required to include health warnings on their packaging and to fund smoking cessation programs. Spare a thought, in particular, for our children and the constant bombardment they experience morning to night. The relentless advertising on television and other media is blindingly obvious, but its effects are not always noticeable, because of how subtle some marketing tricks can be. Next time you're in a grocery store, look at children's breakfast cereal. All of the top 10 brands of children's cereal feature the faces of cartoon characters on the box. But take a closer look and you'll see that the eyes of the characters look down at an angle of about 10 degrees, so that they make eye contact with a 10-year-old. Eye contact releases the trust hormone oxytocin in our brains, and this builds trust with a brand, which leads to higher sales volume, or so the theory goes. Subtle cues like this can tempt children, the most innocent of victims, to choose one brand over another, or to nag Mom or Dad to do so. Yet, as adults, we are hardly any more equipped to deal with such temptations.

Here are other examples of temptations that people cite as reasons for not changing their habits:

- Binge-watching a new series on Netflix or Amazon. Entertainment often lures us away from physical activity and sleep. Netflix hates when we sleep, and so they invented auto play to cue up the next episode without our having to lift a finger!

- Eating fast food. Hard to resist because it tastes good and is cheap and convenient. There goes our healthy eating plan, as we satisfy our addiction to the sugar, salt, and fat crammed into fast food.
- Consumerism. Many of us are greedy consumers and fall prey to the desire to acquire, for example, the latest high-tech gadget. There goes our budget.
- Easy credit. Have you ever signed up for one of those easy-enrollment credit cards? Or bought something because there was zero interest for six months? The temptation is to fund more purchases now, expecting we will have the money later to pay for it all. Total financial sabotage.

Social media has only served to ratchet up the temptation level. Facebook, Twitter, Snapchat, and a host of news and celebrity gossip websites all vie for our time and attention. According to Deloitte, the average person checks his or her cell phone 46 times a day. You may feel that, as we do, in your personal experience that it is much much higher. It won't be long before companies find a way to market to us while we sleep. Consider the Tetris Effect, a syndrome in which persistent thoughts you've had during the day "infect" your dreams—so named because people hooked on playing the game Tetris for hours on end may even dream about fitting the shapes together. Well, that's pretty much what's going on in our brains already, but instead of Tetris, it's the myriad social media sites, adverts, and people that distract us all day long.

But now let's ask how Capability, Motivation, Barriers, and Temptation work together.

The Habit Creation Formula

Capability, Motivation, Barriers, and Temptations are the four forces we've encountered that explain why it's easy or hard for people to adopt new habits. We can combine them into a formula that predicts whether you will change your habits.

> **DEFINITION:** If **Capability + Motivation** are greater than **Barriers + Temptations** for a given action, we'll start to take that action. If this formula holds over time, the action will persist and eventually transform into a habit.

We have used this formula diagnostically for many years, and it has proven powerful for understanding how best to ensure success. Examine the formula carefully and you will notice that it is actually a formula for *creating action*, which is why we call it our *habit creation formula*. The key question of this book is, how do we make and keep that formula holding true, for the habits we want in our lives? And how can we make sure it fails for the habits we're trying to quit?

The Four Powers

If the formula for creating habits combines the four forces outlined above, then to ensure that the formula holds true, we must develop matching Powers: distinct powers to increase our capability and our motivation and powers to reduce barriers and temptations. Developing a minimum expertise in all four powers makes it so much easier to create and sustain habits in ourselves and others. So let's examine each of the four powers in turn.

The Power to GROW Capability. We chose the verb "grow" because both competence and confidence are attributes that build up slowly over time and that require nurturing. Generally, the stronger our Capability is, the more resilient it becomes as well, just as a tree grows stronger and more resilient as it develops from a seedling to a sapling to a young tree to a mighty old oak.

The Power to INSPIRE Motivation. "Inspire" means to breathe life into or to fill someone with the urge to do something. Motivation can appear in a second and disappear just as quickly. The on-again-off-again nature of motivation explains why so many New Year's resolutions fail so quickly and why we complain about just not being motivated enough right now. It opens up new opportunities when we realize, for instance, that instead of needing to be permanently motivated to eat healthily, we just need the power to INSPIRE motivation right around the time when we are choosing what to eat.

The Power to OVERCOME Barriers. Since barriers are static and unmoving, we need the power to go over, through, or around them or to find a way to remove or reduce them. In a similar way in which motivation can arrive and disappear in an instant, barriers are often overcome in one act. True, new barriers may continue to appear, but a single barrier is a much more manageable threat to our chosen habits than the temptations we face. For these, we require a different type of power.

The Power to RESIST Temptations. Because temptations are active and dynamic, we need to hone an active set of skills that are themselves dynamic. Resistance implies a continuous and improving ability to deal with a constantly changing (and improving) set of enticements. For instance, as we learn to resist fast food, what do fast-food burger joints do? They offer our children tempting toys to ensure that they beg us to take them back for more. The power to resist such temptation requires a kind of expertise similar to a martial arts practitioner. It takes many more moves, and years of practice, to become invulnerable to most opponents. Temptations (and those who work to create them) usually take advantage of the many biases that humans suffer, and they work partly because they can strike at the many points in our lives when motivation is absent or lagging. Motivation is fleeting, giving temptation the upper hand, making this power perhaps the most important to develop.

A Context Design Tool Kit

The tools of context design are bite-sized influence methods that either increase Capability and Motivation or decrease or eradicate Barriers and Temptation. A comprehensive Context Design tool kit is, therefore, a large collection of influence techniques that are effective in making the habit creation formula come true in one or more contexts. Since we are generally immersed in all four Contexts at all times, we have to ensure that the formula holds true in all four Contexts. In fact, here's the most important insight:

If the habit creation formula fails in just ONE Context, even if it is true in all three of the other contexts, it becomes less likely that new habits will emerge or that new actions will be taken.

For example, let's say you are committed to getting into shape by working out each day. In the Context of the Self, you are confident and capable, and you've addressed the barriers and temptations that you faced. You're lucky enough to work in an office that has an onsite gym 100 steps from your desk. There are showers and lockers in which you store your gym clothes. The Spaces and Systems contexts are well designed to support the habit creation formula for exercising.

In the Social Context you belong to a group of people who work out together, one of whom is even a personal trainer, so you're supported, confident, and competent going to the gym. Most of your colleagues also use the gym, so no one tempts you to go for a long lunch instead.

One morning an urgent request from a client requires an answer by 2:00 p.m. Lunchtime arrives, and you are not finished but calculate that you can make a quick trip to the gym and still meet the deadline. As you get up from your desk, your boss raises her eyebrows, visually signaling the question, "Where do you think you're going?" In an instant, your motivation to act may dissipate. The social pressure from the client and your boss erects an instant barrier. This failure of the formula in the Social Context alone is enough to stop your action—and negatively impact your commitment to exercise as a habit in the longer term. If this were to persist over time, your existing habit of working out would be at risk.

Lasting success requires that you use influence methods in all four contexts in order to increase the likelihood of success, although of course you should work on the contexts where the formula is most at risk of failing. To do that, you may need to deploy more than one influence method at any given time. The graphic below illustrates the idea of the collection of toolboxes required to cover each combination of one of the Four Powers with each of the Four Contexts. Each toolbox contains a set of influence methods that are effective at generating a single power in a single context. For example, the toolbox in the top right-hand corner holds influence methods that are effective at Growing Capability in the Systems Context.

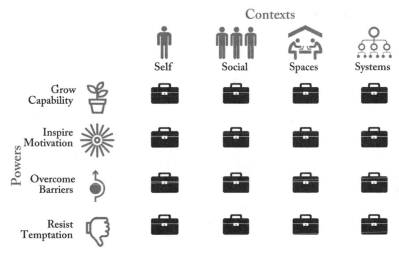

Figure 5.1: The Four Powers Matrix

Influence Methods—The Tools of Context Design

An influence method is any technique that changes one or more of the four forces (Capability and Motivation, Barriers and Temptations) in a way that makes it more likely that the habit creation formula holds true, in at least one Context.

In the following chapters, we'll share many influence methods that we have researched extensively in our BRATLAB. Applying these influence methods is the art and science of designing workplace contexts and, when centered on the right habits, the wellspring of higher performance. The research that helped us develop these methods took us to corporations large and small, casinos, and hospitals and even into the world of street buskers. We observed the interactions between employees and with their customers. Initially, we didn't care whether the influence was positive or negative, whether people became better off or worse off. We were primarily concerned with whether they had been effectively influenced by someone to create a new action or a new habit.

Armed with a long list of successful influence methods, we then turned to the academic research to understand why these methods are so effective. We asked, "Which human biases, heuristics, or assumptions underlie the success of each method?" We also asked, "Which theory, research, or experiment explains why the method works?" Occasionally, we found the explanation in a single human bias such as the power of reciprocity, our compulsion to reciprocate in kind when someone is generous toward us.

We also looked at the side effects of these methods. How did people feel about them? Did they feel manipulated or controlled? Did they feel cheated and taken advantage of? Did they even notice that they had been influenced? Were they grateful for the experience, loyal to the company or institution, and even active advocates of the cause or the product that influenced them? Where these influence methods had been used by companies on their employees, we asked whether the methods not only were effective at generating new habits but also left employees feeling great about their company. In other words, did employees become highly engaged? Finally, we asked how these methods could be repurposed to create habits other than those to which they were originally applied. As an example, could health clubs help you work out longer by copying influence methods used by casinos to help you lose track of time?

So far, we have found more than 80 distinct influence methods that satisfy the following criteria:

1. They are effective at creating new habits.
2. The reasons why they are effective are well understood and validated by research.

3. The method does not have any unwanted side effects and, if implemented in the right way, creates highly engaged employees.

4. The method can be deployed for a variety of different habits, with the right intent, and aligned to the existing culture (way of doing things around here).

The third criterion above had the biggest culling effect on our original list. To illustrate why, let's consider an extreme case. If I'm your employer and I hold a loaded gun to your head and ask you to exercise, would you? Most people, not surprisingly, agree that they would. How would you feel about the way in which I got you to exercise? Would you feel inspired to stay at the company and continue working hard? Most certainly not.

However, what if, instead of wielding a gun, your employer said, "If you work out once every day for a year, I'll give you a hundred bucks"? How would you then feel about your employer? Maybe a little manipulated or bribed? Would you feel any different if they had said, "I will donate $100 to the charity of your choice"? Finally, what if your employer simply asked you to exercise on the basis that it would make you healthier and more productive and would be taken into account when the next round of promotions is being considered? All of these methods leave you feeling a different way, and these differences are highly predictive of how you will act going forward, especially when the influence method is no longer present.

When poor influence methods are used and then removed, we often behave at even lower levels of the targeted habit just to spite the people who used such a ham-fisted and unappreciated tactic on us. We resist being bribed and manipulated or threatened. So, we eliminated from our toolboxes the influence methods that worked in the beginning but did not sustain permanent habit change.

The outcome is a set of influence methods that leaves people thrilled by the experience, grateful for the support, and highly engaged with you as their employer. In the following chapters we will explore some of these influence methods, as we examine each Context. The individual influence methods are like the Lego blocks from which we can build effective strategies to create the habits that drive our destiny. In practice, we often utilize a combination of influence methods that form a cohesive influence strategy.

So let's recap. Our habit creation formula focuses on the four contexts within which we live our lives: Self, Social, Spaces, and Systems. Within these four contexts we have to put the four powers to work: Grow Capability, Inspire Motivation, Overcome Barriers, and Resist Temptations to change the forces acting on us and thus to create changes in our behavior that lead to new habits over time. In the following chapters we will dig deep into the contexts and powers and outline the methods that we have found most successful—beginning with the Context of the Self.

References

Bandura, A. (1977). *Social learning theory*. Englewood Cliffs, NJ: Prentice-Hall.

Bandura, A. (1977). Social learning theory. In B. B. Wolman & L. R. Pomroy (Eds.), *International encyclopedia of psychiatry, psychology, psychoanalysis, and neurology* (Vol. 10). New York: Van Nostrand Reinhold.

Bandura, A. (1997). *Self-efficacy: The exercise of control*. New York: W. H. Freeman/Times Books/Henry Holt (p. 382). Retrieved from http://www.uky.edu/~eushe2/Bandura/banconfidence.html

Christakis, N. A., & Fowler, J. H. (2009). *Connected: The surprising power of our social networks and how they shape our lives*. New York: Little, Brown and Co.

Deloitte. (2017). Global mobile consumer survey: The dawn of the next era in mobile (US edition). Retrieved from https://www2.deloitte.com/us/en/pages/technology-media-and-telecommunications/articles/global-mobile-consumer-survey-us-edition.html

Ericsson, K. A., Krampe, R. T., & Tesch-Romer, C. (1993). The role of deliberate practice in the acquisition of expert performance. *Psychological Review, 100*(3), 363–406.

Musicus, A., Aner, T., & Wansink, B. (2014). Eyes in the aisles: Why is Cap'n Crunch looking down at my child? *Environment & Behavior, 47*(7), 715–733. doi:10.1177/0013916514528793

Polivy, J., C., Herman, P., & Deo, R. (2010). Getting a bigger slice of the pie: Effects on eating and emotion in restrained and unrestrained eaters. *Appetite, 55*(3), 426–430. doi:10.1016/j.appet.2010.07.015

Rotter, J. (2018). The social learning theory of Julian B. Rotter. Retrieved from http://psych.fullerton.edu/jmearns/rotter.htm

Sinichi, A. (2015). What is the Tetris Effect? Retreived from http://www.healthguidance.org/entry/17147/1/What-Is-the-Tetris-Effect.html

Volkow, N. (2014). Why do our brains get addicted? Retrieved from https://www.youtube.com/watch?v=Mnd2-al4LCU

6

The Context of the Self: Managing our Mind-Sets

When we are no longer able to change a situation, we are challenged to change ourselves.

—Viktor E. Frankl

The context that is often the most difficult to change is that of the Self. We are quite adept at noticing the behavior of others but often fail to recognize our own behavior and the causes thereof.

Learning and talent development specialist Dr. Samineh I. Shaheem expresses it well: "Humans are experts at self-deception and engage in this practice on a regular basis. **We recruit an impressive collection of cognitive strategies and behavioral tactics to avoid** the truth and embrace deluded delights. It's much easier to detect it in others because we do it so often that sometimes we're not even aware of doing it."

A study published in *Mayo Clinic Proceedings* supports that view. According to the study, only 2.7 percent of the US adult population practices four cornerstone habits of a healthy lifestyle: a good diet, moderate exercise, maintaining a recommended body fat percentage, and being a nonsmoker. And yet more than 60 percent of Americans claim that they practice all four habits at the recommended rates. Unfortunately, as we all know, self-control frequently fails. Part of the problem is we overestimate our capacity for self-control and the ability to resist temptation.

The individual capacity to change habits is influenced by an individual's thoughts, feelings, perceptions, and mind-set, which are not always that easy to notice or change. It requires awareness, a beginner's perspective, a sense of autonomy, and the confidence to continuously practice in the face of failure:

- Awareness includes understanding our identity and our signature strengths, as well as recognizing underlying motivations. We should continuously strive to achieve a deeper level of self-awareness and identify and use our character strengths to uncover the motivations behind our actions.

- A beginner's perspective allows us to adopt a growth mind-set that encourges us to learn or try new things, push ourselves out of our comfort zones, accept that learning comes from deliberate practice, and respond constructively to useful feedback from others.

- A sense of autonomy in life and at work, using failures and setbacks as opportunities to learn and regain control over out-of-control situations, is a vital trait.

- Confidence relates to a person's belief that he or she can do something or achieve something. Progress is achieved by using small wins to gain confidence, to learn by doing, and to transfer your confidence in one area of your life to another.

We will now explore how we might design the context of the Self using the four powers of Capability, Motivation, Barriers, and Temptations. Said more simply, let's explore ways in which we can change our mind-sets to make the formula for creating habits come true!

Helping Individuals Grow Their Capability

Where do we think control over an event resides? Who or what is responsible for what happens? Are we responsible, or does something outside of ourselves determine the outcome?

In a famous study, patients about to undergo cardiac surgery were split into three groups. The first group had people pray for them but didn't know it. The second group had no one pray for them. The third group was told that prayers were being said for them. The group that had the worst outcome? The third group. This has nothing to do with the power of prayer or lack thereof. Instead, when patients knew that people were praying for them, they viewed their condition as more serious, and their locus of control shifted from internal to external ("in God's hands"). The moral of the story is that, by all means, pray for people who are sick, but don't tell them! Why? Because you leave them lacking agency in their recovery, and that's not good for their expected outcomes.

With an internal locus of control, responsibility rests with us; with an external locus, it rests with someone or something else. People who have an external locus of control tend to have a fixed mind-set;

they believe they cannot change. People who have an internal locus of control usually have a growth mind-set—and, because they believe that they can change, they have control. The message: practice becoming a person with an internal locus of control. By doing so you will reduce stress in your life. And from a habit-forming perspective you will be more likely to persist and overcome barriers than someone with an external locus of control.

Traveling the road to change requires that you know where you're going and set goals for how to get there. But it all starts with believing that you have the power to take the first steps and to keep going when times get tough. When setting goals, it is important that some are small, incremental, and based on very short time frames, so that they are doable stepping-stones en route to larger, more challenging goals. Every time people achieve a smaller goal, it's a reminder of their progress, an acknowledgment of their success, and a motivator to keep moving forward. Take care not to establish only big, unrealistic goals at the beginning, because they can quickly seem out of reach and therefore can be demoralizing. It's better to set daily small goals than large annual goals. This is why so many people fail at achieving their New Year's resolutions. Of course, a combination of both is optimal: small goals to maintain motivation, large goals to ensure that we have an end in mind.

Another way to foster success is to make your goals public: don't keep them to yourself. Announcing your goals can elevate both their importance and your commitment to keep going until you accomplish them. Which is where social media can be brought into play—a simple and effective tactic to broadcast your determination to the wider world. A word of warning: sometimes, declaring goals publicly could have the opposite effect because our mind is tricked into believing that once we've declared our goals, they're as good as achieved. Be sure to follow through with disciplined actions, and don't let speaking about it as if it's done trick your mind into thinking it is done. The best way to avoid this trap is to recruit people in your network to help hold you accountable.

When you're helping other people set and achieve their goals, you can maximize their chances of success by issuing clear, easy instructions to help reduce the perceived difficulty of a task. And keep it simple. The less complex the instructions are, the clearer they are and the more likely it is that people will follow them. Reiterate them, and then let people know how they're doing, often and usefully.

Providing the right kind of feedback is not only a valuable guide to our progress but also a powerful motivator. Professor Benjamin Bloom, one of the foremost researchers on human performance, points out that throughout history every great learning environment has contained a feedback-corrective process in which proficiency was assessed, corrective feedback given, and then another attempt made.

Feedback is even more important than having a goal, as it can direct you toward progress, even if you don't know exactly where you're going to end up. Positive, constructive feedback is inherently motivating, while goals in themselves may not be motivating. Nobel laureate Daniel Kahneman, in his book *Thinking, Fast and Slow*, describes how humans achieve mastery only when their efforts receive frequent and immediate feedback. Says Kahneman, "The acquisition of skills requires a regular environment, an adequate opportunity to practice, and rapid and unequivocal feedback about the correctness of thoughts and actions." That's his prescription for deliberate practice.

You can't develop mastery of anything just by studying a theory or a concept or by watching someone else perform. The best course of action is to pursue a structured and actionable system such as the classic five-step program designed by University of California–Berkeley researchers Stuart and Hubert Dreyfus. In their plan, you first start as a novice learning to recognize features of a skill and acquiring the rules for putting them into action. Second, after gaining experience, you develop competence. Third, with continued practice, you become proficient. At the fourth step, you've become expert and intuitively perform tasks until, finally, at the fifth step, you become a master able to instantly and expertly perform a correct action. It's not something that happens overnight. Malcolm Gladwell, in his book *Outliers: The Story of Success*, says that it takes 10,000 hours of practice to become a master. Says Gladwell, "Practice isn't the thing you do once you're good. It's the thing you do that makes you good." But we can come a lot closer to mastery in a lot less time if we are very deliberate about the way in which we practice.

Of course, it is also essential to put into practice what we've learned. We learn by doing and by getting feedback. This is why *deliberate practice* is so important. You don't improve your golf swing, for instance, by aimlessly hitting balls thousands of times at a driving range without taking time to analyze what you're doing. Deliberate practice, in contrast, is focused. You review and critique what worked and what didn't. You get constant feedback, preferably from a third-party coach or qualified practitioner, because learning is much more effective when you can relate to someone who is already a proven expert or champion whose example or guidance is both instructive and motivational. And there's much more you can do to inspire motivation.

Ways to Inspire Individual Motivation

Why do you exist? Why does your company exist? What's your purpose? Those who answer the question of *why* they do what they do are better able to inspire others to join their cause and create the environment for them to stay loyal and committed. Says international best-selling author Simon Sinek, "When people are financially invested, they want a return. When people are emotionally invested, they want to contribute." Daniel Pink, in his book *Drive: The Surprising Truth about What Motivates Us*, tells us that purpose is "the yearning to do what we do in the service of something larger than ourselves." When an organization is purpose-driven, employees not only have a clear understanding of their goals but also take pleasure in meeting them.

Discovering your genuine or true purpose and communicating it effectively requires authenticity. For an organization, that means your purpose is so ingrained that it is felt and enacted by every member of your team. You'll know you have shared purpose when team members display their excitement to get to work each day and pursue your shared mission. This, of course, requires leadership. And authentic leaders must walk the talk. Oklahoma City mayor Mick Cornett is a superb example. After his city was described as the eighth fattest in America, he decided to take action and bluntly declared, "This city is going on a diet." He did so with style on New Year's Eve while standing in front of an elephant at the local zoo. (Quite a prop!) Cornett's inspiring leadership set in process a chain of events that led to his citizens losing one million pounds, as they followed his personal lead of losing weight.

Having a sense of purpose, knowing your "why," and being able to distinguish between events in life and the meaning we attach to them are all important. An earthquake happens. The sun rises. People get married and divorced. These are events in life, but the meaning of these events is personal and different for each person experiencing them. Joseph Campbell eloquently stated, "Life is without meaning. You bring the meaning to it."

Victor Frankl, World War II concentration camp survivor, one of the giants of modern psychology, and author of the influential *Man's Search for Meaning*, found that people who had deep meaning in their lives were more likely to emerge alive from the camps, as well as being physically and mentally healthier. Those who were devoid of meaning lost hope and were more likely to perish. By understanding and using the power of meaning, we're able to generate positive energy that can be harnessed to help people succeed in any endeavor. Finding deep meaning in life is one of the keys to fulfillment. What does that have to do with habits? Well, since we add the meaning to life, if we decide that forming a new habit is very meaningful to us or the people we care about, versus something trivial, it can provide not only motivation to succeed but also determination in the face of barriers. In fact, meaning often transforms barriers (that we hate) into challenges (that we relish).

Once you have established your personal "why" or your organization's "why" and clearly communicated it, always challenge yourself and your team to do better. But make sure you strike the right balance. People generally set goals that aren't challenging enough in order to avoid the risk of failure. So stretch beyond your comfort zone. A challenge represents an opportunity for improvement. This is in apparent contrast to the advice of setting small, achievable goals to build confidence. But the difference here is how we relate to the goals. If goals occur for us as hard, small and incremental goals are best. If goals occur for us as challenges, then go ahead and put them a little out of your reach so that you have to stretch yourself. It's the framing that makes the difference. Why?

Because when we frame things as a personal challenge and then we succeed, we benefit by:

- Redefining what we think of ourselves (in some sense "better").
- Redefining what we perceive others think of us (more "heroic" in some way).
- Improving our confidence to take on bigger challenges.

The more we challenge ourselves and succeed, the more we are ready to take responsibility for our actions and the results we produce. In fact, that's what we all seek: the autonomy to control our jobs, our careers, and our lives.

Empowering your employees to be independent and to make decisions for themselves can pay off handsomely. A Cornell University study of 320 small businesses, for instance, discovered that companies giving workers some autonomy grew at four times the rate of control-oriented firms and had a third of the employee turnover. The workers were demonstrably happier and more productive. You can also follow Google's example. Cofounders Larry Page and Sergey Brin famously allow engineers to spend 20 percent of their time working on projects that are their own ideas. When Google went public, they cited this approach as being instrumental in the company's ability to innovate, and it has been responsible for significant product developments such as AdSense, a key driver of revenue for Google.

Whatever you do, go out of your way to turn a new habit into something that feels like fun and then motivation levels will soar. Fun is something that provides amusement or entertainment. By definition, it's enjoyable. Beyond that, it's more active and playful. Fun helps people relax and acts as a buffer against stress.

Often fun is simply "enjoyment with surprise." As discussed earlier, scientists have discovered that when the brain can't match new information with data stored in its long-term memory, it releases dopamine, a chemical that stimulates the amygdala, the site of emotion, and unleashes a pleasurable feeling that is associated with the new memory. Result: your employees will become compelled to act. But making work fun is no easy task. In fact, the word "work" brings to mind the opposite of fun. So how can this be achieved? One way is to borrow a page from the gaming industry and "gamify" jobs. How?

By tracking people's progress, letting them earn or lose "points" and "badges" for small wins or losses, and allowing status and cooperation between team players to drive persistence.

In a world where virtual reality and online role-playing games are increasingly an escape for people *from* work, work must fight back by borrowing the tools of gaming to give people the same kind of enjoyment that they get from playing games. Imagine if your employees were addicted to and enjoyed work as much as they do games on their smartphones or Xboxes. Gamifying work is perhaps the most interesting avenue for driving longer-term motivation in employees, because games have dopamine-releasing superpowers. Although this future is arriving quickly, for most of us, work as a game is not quite the reality today.

But even if we and our employees are compelled to act, sometimes things just get in the way of progress. What are the barriers in the context of Self that we must help to destroy or surmount to create change?

Ways to Help Overcome Barriers

First, let's be clear that we can't change reality, but through a method known as cognitive reframing we can observe and understand incidents, ideas, perceptions, and feelings in order to discover more positive options. As Rory Sutherland put it in his TED Talk *Perspective Is Everything*, "Things don't actually much depend on what they really are, but on how we view them."

Individuals with a growth mind-set naturally employ this reframing procedure on a habitual basis, but individuals with a fixed mind-set might find reframing nearly impossible.

- In selling, reframing takes objections and turns them into key reasons to purchase.

- In teaching, reframing explains a point in a different way that might be more understandable to the student.
- In leadership, reframing takes a commonplace or daunting proposal and makes it stimulating.
- In negotiating, reframing can help resolve a conflict by highlighting a novel way to appreciate issues.
- In these ways, reframing is an effective way of turning some barriers, especially the ones we invent in our own stories, into mere irritations or even opportunities.

Someone who believes that he or she has no control over his or her environment will start to act helplessly and ignore any opportunity to boost future prospects. As an example, if you don't get any callbacks from numerous job interviews, you might simply give up and even refuse to act on a golden opportunity when it jumps up and stares you in the face.

Reframing your situation is a way to unlearn helplessness. Shawn Achor, author of *The Happiness Advantage*, came up with the idea of "falling up." Falling up is what separates the successful from those who give up, even when they are overwhelmed or facing adversity. In falling up, you decide how to interpret the situation. A setback becomes an opportunity to learn, not a failure. Practicing learned optimism is a positive psychology approach conceived by University of Pennsylvania professor Martin Seligman—a skill anyone can acquire by purposefully challenging any negative thoughts you might have about yourself. When you catch yourself thinking negatively about yourself or doubting your ability, practice assuming that the opposite is true. There is more than a grain of evidence supporting the effectiveness of faking it until you make it.

Finding the Strength to Resist Temptation

Our ability to invent and share stories differentiates us from every other living thing on this planet and can be used to powerfully resist temptation. Humans are natural storytellers, and we improve or limit our lives through the stories that we tell ourselves. Over time, the stories we tell ourselves become the reality, and if they're negative, they bring the risk of robbing us of happiness, accomplishment, and success. They can also lead people to believe that they have no power to resist temptation or change their circumstances. Someone who constantly tells him- or herself or others "I was a fat kid, so it was inevitable I'd become a fat adult" will find it hard to believe that he or she can change his or her ways and lose weight.

Our identities become shaped by our originating stories, the life stories that are incorporated into the recollections of events and our self-identity. These self-defining memories contribute most to our total sense of who we are. Learning to recognize them can help us gain important insights about our identity, unlearn the helplessness we may have acquired, and begin to restore our self-confidence so that we can better resist temptation.

People are often unaware that they have become stuck in a story of their own creation. They freely use limiting expressions such as "I can't," "I always," "I never," and "That's just who I am." They repeat the same mistakes and attract the same situations and people into their lives. And they become unable to resist temptations.

The language we use can shift us into a new reality and create a new story. Before making a negative statement, such as "I never," "I always," or "I cannot," start with the phrase "Up until now, I have not …" For example, change "I always live from paycheck to paycheck," to "Up until now, I have lived from paycheck to paycheck." This may sound basic, but it is very powerful. As we have discussed, there is a part of us that listens to everything we say and reacts accordingly. So let's change our stories (our beliefs about ourselves, our past, and our present) and then retell them to ourselves and others. In doing so we regain faith and set the wheels in motion to change our lives and resist the temptations that have dictated our behaviors.

Here are some ways to offer support to a person in retelling (and living) his or her new story:

- **Peer coaching and champions:** Having a buddy or someone else who inspires "positive jealousy" can create the right kind of motivation. This person should be a peer, someone comparable for whom the statement "If he or she can do it, so can I" is believable.

- **Goal setting:** Sharing new goals is a new story. Making it public, as we've suggested, enhances your drive to achieve the goals—if you're careful about how you share your goals. Goal setting should be accompanied by action statements such as "I will do this" alongside the statement "This is a goal that I've set for myself." Setting and sharing the goal should not feel like the achievement.

- **Dress for success:** Research shows that people's clothing can directly affect how they think and their behavior. The concept, called "enclothed cognition," can be used to encourage different behaviors through a change of clothing. Dressing for success is not just a phrase but a story that raises our performance.

- **Have great expectations:** There is a psychological phenomenon called the Pygmalion Effect, which is a type of self-fulfilling prophecy. If you think something will happen, you may unconsciously make it happen through either your actions or inaction. Let me give you an example. There were twin brothers whose father was an alcoholic and physically abused them. As adults, one brother became a successful businessman who used his hard-earned money to help abused individuals. The other brother became addicted to drugs and alcohol. The first brother credited his upbringing with making him work hard and then help others who had suffered like he had. The second brother blamed his upbringing for leading him into a life of addiction. The twins perceived their situations differently and constructed different life stories. One brother saw his earlier life as a motivating force that enabled him to succeed; the other brother saw it as an excuse and blamed his father for all of his problems.

It's only natural to doubt your ability to accomplish something from time to time. And that's entirely healthy. But if self-doubt rules your life, it can impede relationships and careers, generating anxiety and depression. Building self-confidence is a proven way to release self-doubt, but it requires you to look at yourself differently and start believing in the qualities that you have. Here are a few ways to get rid of doubt:

- **Distance antagonists:** Stay away from toxic people whose negativity will sow the seeds of your self-doubt. Instead, surround yourself with people who offer support and encouragement and who have a "can-do" mind-set.
- **Recall successes:** It's human nature to remember negative events. Instead, make a point of recalling positive events. Write down your accomplishments—big and small—and review them when doubt clouds your life.
- **Give permission to try again:** Don't think you have to get everything right the first time. That's the path to doubt.

Just know that you can try again (and again, if necessary) and give yourself explicit permission to keep trying.

- **Avoid stress:** Here's another good reason to try to keep stress out of your life: stress makes unwanted thoughts and doubts come back stronger, and when we're tired, stressed, or depressed, our lack of energy leads to self-doubt.
- **Self-affirmation:** Self-affirmation involves thinking about our positive traits and beliefs and has been found to increase confidence and self-control.

Psychologist Albert Bandura once said, "People need enough knowledge of potential dangers to warrant action." Once people are aware of those external forces, they need to be shown how to translate their concerns into effective actions. And what are those external forces? They're the temptations that surround us all day, every day.

They run the gamut from appetizing yet unhealthy fast foods to a variety of products sneakily placed in TV shows and movies to persuade us of their superiority over other products. (Don't believe it? Sales of Reese's Pieces soared 65 percent after "starring" in the movie *E.T. the Extra-Terrestrial.* Sales of Red Stripe beer increased 50 percent after placement in the movie *The Firm*). External forces include all forms of social media that grab our attention away from things we're supposed to be doing or are committed to doing. How many times a day, for instance, do you interrupt a work project to check Facebook and Twitter? External forces also include friends, relatives, and colleagues who seek to influence you one way or another.

Open your eyes and become aware of these temptations and acknowledge them. That's the first step toward being able to resist them. Training ourselves to avoid paying attention to stimuli or cues that promise a reward is one route to regaining self-control.

Habit change is hard. We may be resolute in our decision to start a new habit or quit an old one but then quickly get derailed because our decision to change a habit is often made inside a vacuum, without regard for all of the potential barriers and temptations. Inevitably, external circumstances immediately get in the way and take us off track. These circumstances are actually the four contexts in which we live and work, and they can play an active role in our habit change efforts, whether helping us to succeed or ensuring that we fail.

So now that we've covered the most personal context, the Context of the Self, let's move on to the context of other people, or the Social Context.

References

Achor, S. (2010). *The happiness advantage: The seven principles of positive psychology that fuel success and performance at work*. New York: Broadway Books.

Appel, H. J. C., & Gerlach, A. L. (2015). The interplay between Facebook use, social comparison, envy, and depression. *Current Opinion in Psychology, 9*, 44–49. doi:10.1016/j.copsyc.2015.10.006

Appel, H. J. C., & Gerlach, A. L. (2015). Social comparison, envy, and depression on Facebook: A study looking at the effects of high comparison standards on depressed individuals. *Journal of Social and Clinical Psychology, 34*(4), 277–289. doi:10.1521/jscp.2015.34.4.277

Asch, S. E. (1956). Studies of independence and conformity. I. A minority of one against a unanimous majority. *Psychological Monographs: General and Applied, 70*(9), 1–70.

Bandura, A. (1977). *Social learning theory*. Englewood Cliffs, NJ: Prentice-Hall.

Bandura, A. (1977). Social learning theory. In B. B. Wolman & L. R. Pomroy (Eds.), *International encyclopedia of psychiatry, psychology, psychoanalysis, and neurology* (Vol. 10). New York: Van Nostrand Reinhold.

Bandura, A. (1997). *Self-efficacy: The exercise of control*. New York: W. H. Freeman/Times Books/Henry Holt & Co.

Bloom, B. S. (Ed.). (1956). *Taxonomy of educational objectives: the classification of educational goals. Handbook I: cognitive domain*. London: Longmans.

Carruthers, H. R., Morris, J., Tarrier, N., & Whorwell, P. J. (2010). The Manchester Color Wheel: development of a novel way of identifying color choice and its validation in healthy, anxious and depressed individuals. *BMC Medical Research Methodology, 10*, 12.

DeVaro, J. (2006). Teams, autonomy, and the financial performance of firms. Retrieved from http://digitalcommons.ilr.cornell.edu/articles/107/

Dreyfus H., & Dreyfus, S. (1986). *Mind over machine: The power of human intuitive expertise in the era of the computer*. New York: Free Press.

Frankl, V. E. (1984). *Man's search for meaning: An introduction to logotherapy*. New York: Simon & Schuster.

Gladwell, M. (2008). *Outliers: The story of success*. New York: Little, Brown and Company.

Gokhale, S. V. (2010). Comparative study of the practice of product placement in Bollywood and Hollywood movies. Master's thesis, paper 3860.

Kahneman, D. (2011). *Thinking, fast and slow*. New York: Farrar, Straus and Giroux.

McIntyre, C. K., & Roozendaal, B. (2007). Adrenal stress hormones and enhanced memory for emotionally arousing experiences. In F. Bermúdez-Rattoni (Ed.), *Neural plasticity and memory: From genes to brain imaging*. Boca Raton, FL: CRC Press/Taylor & Francis. Retrieved from https://www.ncbi.nlm.nih.gov/books/NBK3907/

McRaney, D. You are now less dumb. Retrieved from https://www.youtube.com/watch?v=MtPPaCBJdw0

Mick Cornett, M. (2006–2007). This city is going on a diet. Retrieved from http://www.thiscityisgoingonadiet.com/

Moussaïd, M., Kämmer, J. E., Analytis, P. P., & Neth, H. (2013). Social influence and the collective dynamics of opinion formation. *PLoS ONE, 8*(11), e78433. doi:10.1371/journal.pone.0078433

Nordgren, L., van Harreveld, F., & van der Pligt, J. (2009). The restraint bias: How the illusion of self-restraint promotes impulsive behavior. *Psychological Science, 20*, 1523–1528. Retrieved from https://www.ncbi.nlm.nih.gov/pubmed/19883487

Paige, L., & Brin, S. (2004). 70-20-10 rule in Founder Letter. Retrieved from https://abc.xyz/investor/founders-letters/2004/

Phares, E. J. (1965). Internal-external control as a determinant of amount of social influence exerted. *Journal of Personality and Social Psychology, 2*(5), 642–647.

Pink, D. H. (2009). *Drive: The surprising truth about what motivates us.* New York: Riverhead Books.

Rosenthal, R., & Jacobson, L. (1968). Pygmalion in the classroom. *Urban Review, 3*, 16–20. doi:10.1007/BF02322211

Rotter, J. B. (1966). Generalized expectancies for internal versus external control of reinforcement. *Psychological Monographs, 80*, 1–28.

Seligman, M. E. P. (2006). *Learned optimism: How to change your mind and your life.* New York: Vintage Books.

Sinek, S. (2009). *Start with why: How great leaders inspire everyone to take action.* New York: Portfolio.

Shaheem, S, I. (2017). Sincerity of self-deception. Huffington Post. Retrieved from https://www.huffingtonpost.com/dr-samineh-i-shaheem-/sincerity-of-self-deception_b_9246296.html

Smit, E. (2016). U.S. adults get failing grade in healthy lifestyle behavior. Retrieved from http://oregonstate.edu/ua/ncs/archives/2016/mar/us-adults-get-failing-grade-healthy-lifestyle-behavior

Sutherland, R. (2011). Perspective is everything. Retrieved from https://www.ted.com/talks/rory_sutherland_perspective_is_everything?language=en

Wilgress, L. (2016). Pre-school children spend more than four hours a day looking at a screen (Ofcom study). Telegrapgh UK. Retrieved from http://www.telegraph.co.uk/news/2016/11/16/children-are-now-spending-more-time-online-than-watching-televis/

7

The Social Context: Harnessing the Power of Social Contagion

Life's most persistent and urgent question is, "What are you doing for others?"

—Martin Luther King Jr.

The Social Context is made up of everyone with whom you interact each day and the influence they bring to bear on your life, and yours on theirs. At work this means your coworkers and managers and your direct reports. The Social Context is about relationships, the way in which we connect with others, and it often requires the ability to move beyond the self and give priority to the needs of the group. It is constantly influenced by our culture, social norms, the habits of others, and the human networks we construct around us. Consciously designing our Social Context is an immensely powerful way to influence our own behavior.

As in the previous chapter, we will now look at methods for the Social Context that can be deployed with the four powers of Capability, Motivation, Barriers, and Temptations.

Grow Capability with the Help of Others

Social contagion is the spread of properties like ideas and habits via social networks in much the same way that disease spreads between people, except it can be much more positive. One person serves as the stimulus for the imitative actions of another. There are two principal kinds of contagion: emotional contagion and behavioral contagion. Both are transmitted through simple exposure—you can "catch" the mood or behavior from another person just by observing it or, strange as it may seem, even by way of a second- or third-hand connection.

Sociologist and physician Nicholas Christakis, known for his research on social networks, found that the risk of becoming obese is exacerbated by the friends we keep. Our risk of being obese is almost 60 percent higher if a friend is obese, 40 percent higher if a sibling or spouse is obese, 20 percent higher if a friend of a friend is obese, and 10 percent higher if a friend of a friend of a friend is obese, even if you don't know that person or the one in between. It's only at a fourth-degree relationship that no effect is observed. Why would this be? It could be that birds of a feather do flock together or that if you see friends eating fast food, your perception of what's acceptable might accommodate fast-food consumption. More likely, it's because habits are infectious and poor eating habits lead to weight gain.

Philosopher and cognitive scientist Dan Bennett talks about ideas that behave as living things and compete in a Darwinian manner for survival. Good ideas, he says, can rapidly spread through society, but dangerous ideas can hijack our minds like parasites and promulgate just as effectively. Even rudeness spreads, as demonstrated in a series of University of Florida experiments. Researcher Trevor Foulk and colleagues discovered that if you are the target of rude behavior or simply witness rude behavior, you're more likely to behave rudely toward others and to evoke hostility and even revenge. It's important, therefore, to be aware of social contagion, particularly in the workplace, and to use its power positively.

We've found that one of the best ways to spread positive social contagion throughout an organization is to initiate a Change Agent program. A Change Agent is an advocate, role model, cheerleader, and business guide who takes the lead in seeding and inspiring the behaviors in others that you want to instill in your business. Change Agents might act as:

- **Connectors** who bring people together.
- **Helpers** who have the time and patience to show others the way and are always ready to listen, help, or support. (This is really valuable to newer employees learning the ropes.)
- **Advisers** who enjoy accumulating and sharing their knowledge.
- **Motivators** who persuade and energize team members to try new activities or to stay focused.
- **Pioneers** who love to spearhead new approaches and test new systems. They clear the way for others to follow.

Some Change Agents consistently perform one or more of these roles, while for others their role and function change as they develop more skill and experience. Train your Change Agents to effectively use smaller pieces of information, one conversation at a time, and encourage everyone to practice what he or she has just learned. Use online social networks—they're excellent vehicles for creating effective and cohesive Change Agent programs.

The individual Change Agents benefit, too. They get the satisfaction and personal pride from helping others. Also, because they are responsible for others, they find that their own willpower increases—an interesting psychological phenomenon.

While Change Agents are dynamite role models, we also learn from the experiences of others, especially people who are of the same age, gender, situation, or skill level—a peer who is similar to me in some identifiable way. When working in a group, we often conclude that "if you can, I can," and so group activities are very effective at creating confidence. Encourage individuals who have mastered a task to mentor their colleagues. However, have them show, not tell. In other words, to be effective they should physically demonstrate how to accomplish a project or task rather than simply issue instructions. Most people learn by watching and doing, not by simply listening.

The mentors can be given specific training in the principles of guided mastery, the confidence-building technique developed by eminent psychologist Albert Bandura. Corporate executives can engineer opportunities where observational learning can take place efficiently and become contagious. Mentors who are natural experts in guided mastery get exceptional results from their peers because they understand the innate abilities and barriers of each individual. As a result, they can design the appropriate small steps to success as well as provide emotional support addressing a wide range of organizational activities including career planning, handling conflict, and exercising leadership skills.

Another favored strategy we recommend is the dynamic of team power. When you have a group of like-minded individuals pulling together to achieve the same goal, the chances of success are greatly enhanced. Arrange group activities and you'll find that participants motivate each other in a way that not only improves performance but also increases enjoyment.

Look at exercise as an example. It's much more fun to go for a five-mile walk with friends than it is going solo. You talk as you walk, and the time passes faster. Social bonds and friendships develop. The social interaction and peer support elevate moods and alleviate stress. Furthermore, a group of people working in concert reduces individual risk, thereby making everyone more comfortable.

The optimal size of a group depends on the function of the group. For instance, a team tasked with problem solving usually consists of five to 12 members. British researcher and management theorist Meredith Belbin, renowned for his writings on teamwork, recommends an ideal group size of eight together with one specialist. That's because a group of fewer than five hampers creativity and limits the number of perspectives, while a group of more than 12 may face increased conflict and spur the formation of splinter groups. The larger the group, the greater the propensity for social loafing and the harder it becomes to establish group norms.

The real value of doing things as a group, however, is that we gain confidence when we are part of a group, which we may lack when tackling a task on our own.

Ever-present throughout the Grow Capability construct is a social activity that largely makes us human: the magic of storytelling. Great storytellers, whether filmmakers, authors, or journalists, move us through emotional connections. They tell stories that help us make sense of the world, remind us of our humanity, and teach us about life. Above all, the best stories are motivating and uplifting. The more powerful the story is, the more we engage, and the more we want to know about the communicator's message.

As the country's leading pioneer in the field of neuroeconomics, Dr. Paul J. Zak studies the neurochemical roots of human decision-making in the context of economic behavior. He has shown that when watching a sad story, two neurochemicals are released: cortisol and oxytocin. The production of cortisol engenders a feeling of distress and encourages the listener to pay attention. Oxytocin, on the other hand, promotes care and connection and stimulates empathy. This, of course, plays a key role affecting an individual's behavior toward others and the quality of social relationships. In many ways, stories are the root of habit change.

We suggest that you think about emotional and transformational stories suited to your business environment that will forge relationships and help stimulate positive experiences.

Creating a Culture That Inspires Motivation

So now that we have explored various methods for growing capability, let's focus on how best to inspire our workforce to become peak performers.

As Stephen Covey says, "Start with the end in mind." With a powerful vision for your company, we're able to set expectations for each individual within our company, expectations for how he or she will contribute toward making that vision a reality. Why is this motivating? Because we like to meet the expectations of other people, especially those in leadership positions.

One of the things that sets expectations of desired behaviors for employees is the culture of our companies. Organizational culture involves a learned set of behaviors that are common knowledge to all participants and embody the values, beliefs, perceptions, and stories about the organization. Leadership must lead. You don't want a situation where leadership says one thing but the actions don't reflect the words. All your written policies, emails, and notices are doomed unless leadership conducts itself in a way that is consistent with the vision and the desired culture. Once you establish the vision, you then:

- Communicate this vision with passion. We're motivated to pursue things that others see as exciting.
- Constantly reiterate the policy both verbally and in writing. Sometimes all it takes to motivate us is a reminder of why our roles are important.
- Make sure leaders model the policy behaviors. We're motivated to act in similar ways as our leaders do, if for no other reason than our belief that this might lead to a promotion or other recognition.
- Share data showing that the majority follows the rules. We're motivated to fit in.
- Sanction those who do not follow the rules. We hate being called out for not performing.
- Align pay and recognition systems to desired habits. Although incentives may not be strong motivators, poor, misaligned, or insulting incentives can crush motivation.

Humans have a need to connect with other humans, a trait that's as fundamental as our need for food and water. Psychologist Matthew D. Lieberman, author of *Social: Why Our Brains Are Wired to Connect*, expresses it well: "The data suggests that we are profoundly shaped by our social environment and that we suffer greatly when our social bonds are threatened or severed. When this happens in childhood it can lead to long-term health and educational problems. We may not like the fact that we are wired such that our well-being depends on our connections with others, but the facts are the facts."

Having a strong social connection is clearly correlated with more positive work attitudes, higher self-esteem, better well-being, a sense of satisfaction, and improved performance, and it promotes active engagement in the organization's mission. Part of establishing that connectivity comes from an understanding of social norms, the largely unwritten rules that guide our behavior in society. In many ways, they are more like social obligations than laws, and they vary from culture to culture. For instance, in the United States, shaking hands with someone you just met and turning off your cell phone in the movie theater are social norms, as is looking someone straight in the eye, while in some countries making direct eye contact is considered rude or threatening behavior. Conforming to social norms greases the wheels of the social interaction that's necessary for acceptance within a group. Conformity also portrays allegiance to the group and ties in with our innate desire for connectedness.

Social support from peers, family, and friends can make all the difference in achieving connectedness, which, in turn, raises an individual's involvement, confidence, motivation, and ability to succeed. Tim Rees and Paul Freeman, in their study "Social Support Moderates the Relationship between Stressors and Task Performance through Self-Efficacy," conclude that social support is important because it:

- Moderates stress.
- Enhances confidence.
- Directly improves task performance.

Participants in their study performed better when they perceived that there was someone there for them to take their mind off things (emotional support), to encourage them and boost their confidence (esteem support), to give them constructive criticism and technical advice (informational support), and to help set up sessions in practice (tangible support). It's no coincidence that that sounds like the definition of a great manager at your workplace!

Teams are excellent structures for developing peer support. A team, through shared purpose, shared rituals, and time spent together, increases cohesiveness of a group, increases commitment, and builds trust. The team is a positive platform where people have a vested interest in a collective destiny when they succeed or fail together.

Overcoming Archetypes and Cliques

It's time to change the conventional view of what constitutes a corporate hero. Traditionally, as we discussed earlier, that accolade goes to those who work longer hours and work extra hard, taking on projects left, right, and center. Research shows that more than one-third of "hero" workers don't leave the office for lunch and more than 50 percent accept the fact that they will do work while on vacation.

Yet the reality is that this kind of behavior only leads to disengagement and ineffective performance, as well as deteriorating health and well-being. For the benefit of the organization, the individual disadvantages him- or herself, negatively impacting personal well-being and family responsibilities. Changing this behavior requires a mandate from the top.

Though the evidence is significant, it may be difficult for people to understand how spending less time working results in higher productivity. A *Harvard Business Review* (HBR) article, headlined "The Research Is Clear: Long Hours Backfire for People and for Companies," says that numerous studies at the Finnish Institute of Occupational Health and elsewhere have found that **overwork and the resulting stress can lead to numerous health problems**, including impaired sleep, depression, heavy drinking, diabetes, impaired memory, and heart disease. That's quite understandable. But working long hours also has horrendous consequences for a company's bottom line, as the result of absenteeism, turnover, and **rising health insurance costs**.

Says the HBR, "Even the Scroogiest of employers, who cared nothing for his employees' well-being, should find strong evidence here that there are real, balance-sheet costs incurred when employees log crazy hours." But it's not just a cost problem. Overworked employees serve customers poorly, and they make bad decisions and many more errors, and these all affect the customer experience, product quality, brand, and reputation and, in the longer term, growth.

All the more reason, therefore, for company leaders to encourage employees to take time to refresh and reenergize. Examples:

- After 90 minutes of work, take a mental and physical break.
- Support energy renewal rituals such as meditation.
- Motivate managers to join midday workout sessions.
- Become a role model for a new hero archetype who practices habits in support of his or her health, happiness, and financial security.

While employees with strong social support groups or "best friends" at work are generally more productive, some social groups or cliques become exclusionary and ferment an us-versus-them culture. This can breed workplace conflict.

Executives can steer culture toward employee engagement, improved performance, workplace happiness, and overall well-being by breaking apart such cliques and castes. In a nationwide CareerBuilder survey of nearly 3,000 workers, 43 percent of respondents said cliques populate their workplace. CareerBuilder's VP of Human Resources, Rosemary Haefner, noting that they can be counterproductive, said, "Regardless of age, cliques form to provide social comfort to its members, but from an organizational perspective, they can stand in the way of big picture goals by preventing collaboration and inclusion of diverse perspectives. While being a member of their 'in group' can provide short-term satisfaction and advantageous connections, the best workers and leaders will ultimately be those who can work and empathize with many different types of people."

In one study, Pinar Acar, a professor of organizational behavior, found that individuals who strongly identify with demographic cliques would choose what was best for the clique rather than what was best for the company. But the formation of cliques is not surprising, says Amy Hoover, president of Talent Zoo: "People are creatures of habit, and the habits you pick up early in life often carry through to adulthood. One of these habits is to group with others who are like-minded or similar to us. It happens at work, at parties, at networking events—any place where there are groups of people." Management actually plays a large part in the development of cliques. Half of workers interviewed in the CareerBuilder survey said that management was part of existing cliques, which increases pressure on employees to participate. Unfortunately, employees who are not part of the clique live with the belief that their privileged peers in the inner circle receive better assignments and higher pay and are always chosen for promotion.

Leadership expert and author Bob Whipple recommends several steps to deter the growth of cliques. They include:

- Be aware of cliques. The first step is to honestly recognize that they exist. It's easy to spot groups who always sit together at lunch or have their own exclusive internal email group.
- Encourage an inclusive culture. Embrace and publicly acknowledge the input of all employees.
- Take a few kingpins aside. There will always be informal leaders who establish themselves as the "Grand Poohbah" of a group and whose ideas carry the most weight. Identify these leaders and ask them to make their group inclusive. One exemplary strategy is to solicit their advice on how to overcome the problem of selectiveness and exclusion in the organization.

- Mix things up in meetings. Rotate seating at meetings, giving employees an unavoidable opportunity to network with others.
- Transplant people. Break up groups by transferring individuals to other projects. Handle this with kid gloves, though, because it can backfire. You can pave the way by cultivating a culture of cross-training.
- Inject new blood. Introduce a newcomer with a strong personality and ideas of his or her own.

Reducing cliques in an office environment has to be done in a subtle manner. Managers should ensure that employees understand that good organizations take the input of all employees seriously. Also, regularly conduct workplace training for supervisors so they understand the value of diversity. Companies must operate a zero-tolerance policy for exclusionary, bullying, and harassing behaviors that naturally force employees to form cliques based on demographic likenesses. Discriminatory behaviors often occur without mal-intent and are preventable if company culture makes awareness and education a priority.

Lack of social support and friendship in the workplace is a significant barrier, yet it's relatively simple to overcome. A strong support structure—friends helping friends—makes individuals more resilient, productive, and content. This was demonstrated in an innovative study at the Carlson School of Management in Minneapolis, in which 26 teams of three friends and 27 teams of three acquaintances were given specific instructions for building Tinkertoy models. The friends constructed an average of nine models, whereas the acquaintances were able to construct an average of only 2.4 models—a significant difference.

If you want to create a new habit, one of the barriers you'll face is fear of going it alone and perhaps even the barrier of not knowing where to get started. If that applies to you, find a club (or start a club) for people wanting to take on the same habit. That way, you can learn from each other, or you can learn from people who are more experienced than you, and they can show you the many easier ways to overcome barriers that will show up for you. That's a lot easier than facing them all on your own or figuring them out the hard way.

Now let's look at how other people can be a source of temptation and distraction, preventing us from creating new habits, and what we can do about it—or, better yet, how we can recruit friends to help us resist temptations.

Resist Temptations Together

Moral licensing is the permission we give ourselves to do something "bad" on the basis that we deserve it because we've done something "good." *Washington Post* writer Michael Rosenwald gave these examples: "We drink Diet Coke with Quarter Pounders and fries at McDonald's. We go to the gym and ride the elevator to the second floor. We install tankless water heaters and then take longer showers. We drive SUVs to see Al Gore's speeches on global warming."

Sometimes, in fact, we do not even wait to do something bad because we plan to be good in the future. We say, "I'll take advantage of the holiday sales because I'll cut back on spending afterward" or "I'm going to start my diet tomorrow, so I can eat whatever I want today." It's easy to see that moral licensing typically has negative consequences and enables problematic behaviors such as procrastination, selfishness, and poor dietary and health habits. We need to catch ourselves indulging in the delusion that is moral licensing. Instead, keep your resolve and you'll find that your self-confidence and self-esteem get a boost. Better yet, if you truly want to change some aspect of your life, developing strong social support networks with people who share your goals will help you accomplish more than going it alone.

Peers can keep us focused on our choices and help us move beyond moments of weakness.

No matter how rational and high-minded we try to be, the effort of continuously making sensible choices by ourselves exerts a toll on our energy resources; this is called decision fatigue. It's different from physical fatigue, as we're not consciously aware of being tired, but we are low on mental energy. Result: the brain becomes inattentive, acting on impulse instead of thinking through the consequences of our actions. Then there is the ultimate energy saver: not doing anything at all, which only creates a greater long-term problem.

Experiments at Case Western Reserve University in Cleveland and at Florida State University demonstrate that there is a finite store of mental energy for exerting self-control. Sharing your challenge and your burdens enhance your willpower. It's one of the principal reasons that attendees at recovery programs such as Alcoholics Anonymous say they are so successful. Go ahead and create an accountability group of empathetic and like-minded peers in your organization. A willpower contract is one in which one person agrees to actively help another person stick to his or her plan and vice versa. Both people are in action, helping each other stay on track in the face of temptation. This connection relies on the fact that we have seemingly unlimited willpower when it comes to telling others what to do but run out of willpower when telling ourselves what to do (or at least when listening to ourselves.)

Knowing how to say no is a skill that we have to develop if we want to live a productive life. Saying no to unnecessary commitments gives us time to pursue endeavors that are meaningful to us. Resisting daily temptations allows us to stay on course to accomplish our goals. But saying no is easier said than done, and when we can't find the words, we often just say yes as a default and get ourselves into trouble as a result.

By scripting and practicing a series of responses to anticipated temptations, we are better able to reject them. Consider, for example, the situation where you're dining with a friend or colleague who orders an alcoholic drink. Pressure from our peers is very influential. It's easier to follow suit, especially if this person implores, "Go on. Just have one."

There are a variety of assertion skills you can deploy to resist this kind of pressure:

- **Humor.** "No thank you. I cannot lose any more brain cells. I need them all."
- **Change the subject.** Propose a different pursuit. "Let's do *x* instead."
- **Walk away.** You might feel obliged to face "the enemy," but often it's easier just to leave.
- **Avoid it.** Sometimes you know in advance that a situation is going to become uncomfortable. So why go there in the first place?
- **Strength in numbers.** If you surround yourself with friends who make good choices, it's easier for you to do the same. The opposite is just as true.
- **Creating empathy.** You could say, "You know, I'm really trying to drink less, and I'm the kind of person who, if I have one, I'll likely have a few drinks. So my request is that you support me in avoiding alcohol for now by not offering me a drink. I don't mind if you drink, but please support me in not drinking."

Think about potential temptations and practice replies that will roll off your tongue and you'll be more confident in deflecting these temptations. One simple method demonstrated in several research studies is to say, "I don't," instead of "I can't." In one of the studies,

30 women in a health and wellness seminar were divided into three groups. Group 1 was instructed to "just say no" when temptation reared its ugly head. Group 2 had to use the "can't" strategy and say, "I can't miss my gym session today." Group 3 had to implement the "don't" strategy: "I don't miss gym sessions." After 10 days, one out of 10 members of the "can't" group (group 2) persevered with their goals, three out of 10 of the "just say no" group (group 1) did the same, while eight out of 10 of the "don't" group were the most successful. Conclusion: saying "I don't" is a must-do.

A simple change of words is meaningful. Our words help to frame our sense of empowerment and control. The words that we use create a feedback loop in our brains that impacts our future behaviors. For example, every time we say "I can't," we create a reminder of our limitations. In comparison, when we say "I don't," we create a feedback loop that reminds us of our control over the situation. It is a phrase that can propel you toward breaking your bad habits and following your good ones.

Another strategy that can be brought into play shows us how to handle life's embarrassing moments. We all get embarrassed from time to time. Sometimes it's self-inflicted, and sometimes it's because of the actions of others. Often, your response might be a mixture of blushing, sweating, anxiety, stumbling over words, and fidgeting. Or you might try to cover up your embarrassment with a nervous laugh, which often happens when you've broken a rule of etiquette. On the other hand, if you feel the situation is serious, you might get angry and lash out. What's important is learning how to control your reaction so that you can stabilize emotional responses in social environments, strengthening your resolve to resist temptation. Learning to deal with the embarrassment of a failure is a way to handle the temptation to just give up.

And take heart. Surprisingly, far fewer people than you think actually notice your "embarrassing" mistake. And those who do don't judge you as harshly as you think. Knowing this can soothe the apprehension that's inherent in all social exchanges. Thinking that people judge you more harshly than they do is a form of self-deception known as the Spotlight Effect. It was spotlighted (!) in a Cornell University study in which 109 men and women had to go into a crowded room wearing a T-shirt bearing Barry Manilow's face. They were very uncomfortable doing so (apparently the singer is not universally worshipped) and felt that most of the other people in the room paid undue attention to them. The reality was that less than a quarter of people even noticed the T-shirt.

Knowing that you're probably blowing the embarrassment out of proportion helps. As psychologist Kenneth Savitsky says, "You can't completely eliminate the embarrassment you feel when you commit a faux pas, but it helps to know how much you're exaggerating its impact." The same is true when we fail to stick to a habit and feel embarrassed by that failure.

You can prepare for future embarrassments by engaging in a practice called "constructive embarrassment." The theory is that if you deliberately immerse yourself in an embarrassing situation, you learn how to react when similar situations arise. By taking part in uncomfortable activities, you can break down your fears. Embrace the humiliation! This means seeking out opportunities for embarrassment: perhaps public speaking or making an office presentation or stepping onto the dance floor—anything where you think you might make a fool of yourself. When you make that embarrassing mistake, don't dwell on it. Get over it. And rest assured that when you prepare yourself for embarrassment, it rarely happens. If it does happen, the fact that you've already anticipated that possibility makes it easier to accept.

Now that we've tackled the ways to handle life's embarrassments, let's turn to the subject of envy—one of the seven deadly sins and another of life's temptations. Envy is not as bad as it is made out to be and can be used positively in spite of the fact that most people feel it's a virtue to admire and a vice to be envious. While admiring someone feels positive, it may not motivate you to improve yourself, whereas being envious feels frustrating and, as such, may stimulate the intent to do better and resist behaviors that might get in your way of successfully creating habits.

It may seem counterintuitive, but positive envy could become the driving force behind our successes. As Art Markman, psychology professor at the University of Texas–Austin, says, "When you are happy with your performance, then it is hard to be motivated to work harder and to do more. Instead, you must suffer some discomfort to push yourself to a higher level of achievement. Athletes often do this by finding a rival and setting the goal to outwork that rival."

The same attitude can be employed in the often-cutthroat world of business. Says Markman, "There are two ways to apply it. First, looking at the success of rival companies can help galvanize motivation within a company to achieve a new goal. Second, when individuals within a company focus on what they have not yet achieved in their careers, it spurs them to want to move upward through the organization."

Instead of resenting another person's success, we can work diligently to attain the same for ourselves. Instead of complaining, we can use these jealous feelings to tackle a new challenge. Envy can uncover what we want and provide the energy to resist temptations that lead us away from achieving it.

Human beings necessarily depend on one another, even more so when we are striving to create, and especially sustain, new habits. We often have to rely on the strength of others while on our journey of habit creation. When we fail, grow weary, or simply stop paying attention, those around us must be primed to respond and bring us back on track. We should try to be that for others too. Empathetically connecting to share willpower, encourage, remind, and be a contribution to the lives of others all have a happy way of generating positive payback.

References

Acar, F. P. (2014). Social identification and altruism in diverse teams. *European Journal of International Management, 8*, 55-72. doi:10.1504/EJIM.2014.058484

Baard, P. P., Ryan, R. M., & Deci, E. L. (2004). Intrinsic need satisfaction: A motivational basis of performance and well-being in two work settings. *Journal of Applied Social Psychology, 34*(1), 2045–2068.

Bandura, A. (1994). Self-efficacy. In V. S. Ramachaudran (Ed.), *Encyclopedia of human behavior* (Vol. 4, pp. 71–81). New York: Academic Press. (Reprinted in H. Friedman [Ed.], *Encyclopedia of mental health*. San Diego: Academic Press, 1998).

Belbin, R. M. (2012). *Team roles at work*. Abingdon, Oxon: Routledge.

Buettner, D. (2012). *The blue zones: 9 lessons for living longer from the people who've lived the longest*. Washington, DC: National Geographic Partners.

Carey, B. (2003). It's not all about you. *Los Angeles Times*.

Christakis, N. A., & Fowler, J. H. (2013). Social contagion theory: Examining dynamic social networks and human behavior. *Statistical Medicine, 32*, 556–577. doi:10.1002/sim.5408

Dennett, D. C. (2003). *Freedom evolves*. London: Penguin.

De Pater, I. E., Van Vianen, A. E., & Bechtoldt, M. N. (2010). Gender differences in job a challenge: A matter of task allocation. *Gender, Work & Organization, 17*, 433–453. doi:10.1111/j.1468-0432.2009.00477.x

Foulk, T., Woolum, A., & Erez, A. (2016). Catching rudeness is like catching a cold: The contagion effects of low-intensity negative behaviors. *Journal of Applied Psychology, 101*(1), 50-67.

Gagne, M., & Deci, E. L. (2005). Self-determination theory and work motivation. *Journal of Organizational Behavior*, 26, 331–362.

Green, C. S. (2015). The research is clear: long hours backfire for people and companies. *Harvard Business Review*. Organizational Culture. Retrieved from https://hbr.org/2015/08/the-research-is-clear-long-hours-backfire-for-people-and-for-companies

Lee, J.H., (2012). Can envy at work be good for you? *Fortune*. http://fortune.com/2012/10/09/can-envy-at-work-be-good-for-you/

Lieberman, M. D. (2013). *Social: Why our brains are wired to connect*. New York: Crown Publishers/Random House.

Losada, M., & Heaphy, E. (2004). The role of positivity and connectivity in the performance of business teams: a nonlinear dynamics model. *American Behavioral Scientist*, 47, 740.

Rees, T., & Freeman, P. (2009). Social support moderates the relationship between stressors and task performance through self-efficacy. *Journal of Social and Clinical Psychology, 28*, 245-264. doi:10.1521/jscp.2009.28.2.24

Rosenwald, M.S. (2010). Why going green won't make you better or save you money. *Washington Post*.

Smith, J. (2013). How to deal with cliques at work. Forbes. Retrieved from https://www.forbes.com/sites/jacquelynsmith/2013/07/25/how-to-deal-with-cliques-at-work/#1e489a447920

Umberson, D., & Montez, J. K. (2010). Social relationships and health: A flashpoint for health policy. *Journal of Health and Social Behavior, 51*(Suppl), S54–S66. doi:10.1177/0022146510383501

Whipple, R. (2009). *Leading with trust is like sailing downwind*. Executive Excellence Publishing.

Zak, P. J. (2015). Why inspiring stories make us react: the neuroscience of narrative. *Cerebrum, 2, 2*.

8

The Spaces Context:
Build for
Good Habits

We shape our buildings,
thereafter they shape us.

—Sir Winston Churchill

Our senses are constantly bombarded with information. But if we pay attention to every little detail in our surroundings, we'd have no mental space left to work on the things we feel are important. The result? Most of what enters our brains never registers in our consciousness, but that doesn't mean it doesn't affect our behavior. That's why the design of the built environment is so very important to help us create good habits.

As an example, our environment clearly impacts the business and financial decisions we make, as shown by an experiment in which people were given $10 to share between themselves and another person. If they were situated in a room with reminders of business, such as a briefcase, a fountain pen, or a leather portfolio, they were twice as likely to keep more of the money for themselves as those in the control group with no business influencers. Asked why they chose the split that they did, all of the participants responded that they just felt it was fair. None of them noticed that the "business items" primed them to think in more of a win/lose way, which is often the mind-set that is present in business negotiations (albeit this mind-set serves no one in the longer term).

The spaces in which many people work—our offices—are mostly designed to be clean, apparently efficient, and sterile. The lines are usually firm and square, the materials industrial and resistant to hard knocks. They are also designed by architects, commercial office furnishers, and landlords, guided by the team in purchasing and facilities management or, in smaller companies, the whims and wishes of a CEO, or the CEO's spouse! And so we get what we get: offices that are configured to look great, last well, or limit risks.

In contrast, companies design their customer service model or their products to attract, delight, and retain customers and grow their business. Great companies think about their customer experience and not just the product or service that they offer. To accomplish that, they find the best experts to conduct market research; perform customer anthropological studies; create, test, and improve experiences along with their products and service; and continue to innovate. But often corporate leaders don't devote the same effort to meet the needs of their employees. Given that employees very often ARE a key element of the customer experience, this is shortsighted for several reasons.

We say we need to attract and retain the best employees. We say we need to engage them, to inspire them to do great work, and to offer them an amazing work experience. But take a look at the spaces in which we ask our employees to work. If we're brutally honest, we will admit that we rarely treat our workplace with the same professional expertise we lavish on our customers.

So let's evaluate how, within the Spaces Context, we can design our physical spaces to support people to act in positive ways, even at a level below their consciousness.

Designing Spaces That Make Good Habits Easy

Most offices spaces are not like Google or other high-tech environments that have embraced cutting-edge, employee-friendly design concepts. Instead, many continue to be cubicle farms that lack life and sensuality and, instead of inspiring us, drain us. But don't worry; it's not necessary to have Google's deep pockets. Designing an office space that enhances your employees' daily existence doesn't have to cost a fortune. Use your imagination. Get creative. Improve your space and make it easy for them to practice good habits and to perform at their best.

Environmental psychologist Judith Heerwagen, coauthor of *Biophilic Design: The Theory, Science and Practice of Bringing Buildings to Life*, suggests some fundamental elements that help foster an environment conducive to collaboration, creativity, innovation, deep thinking, and mentorship. Here they are in brief:

Employee Engagement: Workers are more likely to connect and collaborate if they can see each other. Provide work spaces that enable engagement by allowing visibility, openness, and employee mobility. Prominently display awards and recognition to reinforce employee motivation. By seeing other people work effectively, we gain both confidence and competence.

Temperature Control: Giving workers a measure of personal control over ambient conditions, especially temperature, has been found to increase productivity. Setting the right temperature is associated with less sick time and improved task-related accuracy. It also ensures that we manage our energy. Working in a too-hot office saps energy, and as energy decreases, so does our belief in our abilities. The more exhausted we become, the less energy we have to put in a good day's work or to tackle the habits that restore our energy. A slightly cooler environment keeps us alert and feeling like we can take on more tasks, including good habits.

Access to Nature and Daylight: Views of the natural environment reduce stress and foster a more positive emotional state. Daylight affects well-being and psychological functioning, so endeavor to design a work space to include windows with views and access to outdoor space. If this is not possible, use indoor plants. All of these elements can contribute to better sleep, a key pivotal habit. Our circadian rhythm benefits from getting natural light at the right times during the day, mostly in the morning, and this also boosts our energy and our sleep quality.

Sensory Change and Variability: Limited visual stimulation can dull the senses and affect one's ability to stay alert and focused. Introduce textures and liven up uninspiring areas with color, artwork, and plants. Sometimes, these artifacts can be used to prime moods that are useful for particular tasks. For example, in the Habits at Work offices, we have a space in which a few symbols of danger are present (a red toy fire truck and a stop sign). Why? Because when we are primed for danger, we are more likely to pick up errors in a document. We encourage employees to locate themselves in this area when they're doing work such as proofreading or other tasks that require error detection.

Color: Choose colors to support the behavior you want. Generally, brighter colors are said to promote greater focus and accuracy. Blue is likely to be calming, furthering mental control and clear, creative thinking. Red enhances feelings of strength and energy and is associated with vitality and ambition. But it is also a color that primes for danger, like the fire truck mentioned above. The science of color, however, appears to be a little less reliable than other environmental influences. So, perhaps in this area, it is smart to balance aesthetics and influence science.

Noise Control: Noise is often a source of discontent in the workplace, but, in reality, noise may promote productivity as well as impede it. The key is to cater to personal preferences as much as possible and give individuals some control, with the introduction of doors and acoustic separation. Keep noisy activities away from quieter ones. Noises and people who interrupt work are the death of productivity. Why? Some researchers estimate that it takes as much as 15 minutes to return to full focus once we've been interrupted. If you work in an open-plan office and you're interrupted on average four times per hour, kiss having a productive day goodbye.

Crowding: Minimize the uncomfortable perception of crowding by making spaces light and bright, by opening up high ceilings, or by placing mirrors on walls. Mirrors are a particularly powerful way to influence behavior, as we'll see below.

Indoor Air Quality: Have you heard of Sick Building Syndrome (SBS)? It's a recognized condition linked with time spent in a building that's probably "infected" with inadequate ventilation and chemical pollutants. Improve your air quality and you'll reduce absenteeism caused by respiratory disease, asthma, and allergies. But having a space that doesn't make people sick is the least you should do. Think of how well your engine runs when the air filters are clogged. In the same way, think about how effectively your employees will work if their lungs are hard at work each day clearing out impurities in the air. We don't notice this, of course, but over a long career in a building with stale air, this can surely have an impact not just on our health and well-being but also on our performance.

Use of space can also be applied to encourage healthy choices. This is referred to as Choice Architecture, a term that was coined by Richard Thaler and Cass Sunstein and refers to "the practice of influencing choice by changing the manner in which options are presented to people." When healthy choices are the easy choices, more people will make them and make them more often.

In response to research showing that prolonged sitting may be a significant risk factor for heart disease, companies across America have slowly begun to endorse regular activity and exercising at work, and even while working. Standing desks, walking meetings, or regular brain breaks during the day are becoming commonplace and are making it easier for people to participate in at least some exercise while at work.

When it comes to healthy eating, distance is perhaps even more important. Food travels on average 1,400 miles to get to us, but we often move only a few feet to get to it. Despite people's protestations that they are "foodies," for most people the following rule is true: we eat what's at hand. In some research, a matter of inches can make the difference. When healthy options are raised a few inches above unhealthy options on a shelf, people make better choices. Many companies think they are supporting employees when they install vending machines serving candy and other junk food, but in reality, by putting this kind of food close to employees, they make it really difficult for them to maintain a healthy diet. What should companies do instead?

When you want people to make better choices, you can get better results with a gentle nudge in the right direction rather than directional suggestions or factual assessments. Make sure it's subtle. If the nudge is too obvious or too forceful, it will feel manipulative and reduce trust. Nudging works better when people don't consciously register what's happening. Let me give you some examples to demonstrate the persuasiveness of one's environment.

- The smell of cleaning fluids is likely to motivate people to keep an area clean.
- Add information to electricity bills that shows individuals how much they consume compared to their neighbors and they soon cut back.
- People are tougher negotiators when sitting on hard chairs as opposed to soft chairs.
- You move faster through shopping centers when faster music is playing.
- See what I mean?
- Google transformed its reputation for fattening its employees with a generous food-on-demand program by introducing healthy nudging strategies such as:
- Placing M&Ms in opaque bins instead of clear dispensers, thereby subduing the temptation and making it harder to grab the candy. Result: calorie intake cut by 9 percent in just one week.
- Positioning a salad bar at the entrance to the cafeteria because people tend to fill their plates with what they see first.

- Installing signs stating that people with bigger plates eat more. Result: small-plate usage increased to 32 percent.
- Initiating a traffic signal approach: green labels paired with vegetables and salads and red labels identifying unhealthy or calorie-laden foods such as desserts.
- Putting bottled water at eye level in the fridges and relegating sodas to the bottom. Result: water intake upped 47 percent; calories from unhealthy drinks dropped 7 percent.

Elsewhere, in an experiment at a student campus shop, green footprints were placed on the floor leading toward the fruit shelf, which led to fruit sales skyrocketing by nearly 100 percent. This type of approach can also be used to get individuals on the right track physically. You can connect employees between departments by positioning common usage areas such as water coolers, toilets, or pantries at strategic points. Establishing obvious pathways to these locations encourages relationship building and knowledge sharing.

Other senses including smell and hearing can guide people in the right direction. Researchers at the University of Chicago, for instance, found that 84 percent of shoppers were more attracted to an identical pair of shoes when they were displayed in a pleasant-smelling room versus an odorless room. In a consumer test of shampoos—rating qualities such as easier to rinse out, foaming better, and leaving hair glossier—a product that initially ranked last came first in a subsequent test after its fragrance had been altered.

Music and certain sounds, especially the sounds of nature, have been shown to have a wide range of benefits including elevating mood, reducing the perception of pain, improving sleep quality, increasing workout endurance, and sharpening cognitive performance.

There are visual cues, as well, that optimize our Capability. Signs, for instance, are universal, highlighting immediate and actionable information. They can be understood by people all over the world, making them one of the most effective communication tools at our disposal.

There are some basic rules for what makes a good sign:

- It should be at eye level.
- It should contain symbols and pictures.
- It should contain as few words as possible.
- It should use easily read fonts (sans serif).
- It should use large type.
- It should use the power of nudges (as described earlier).

Now take a look at the following road sign.

Which direction do you think people will follow? Pictures are more powerful than words—so people typically "obey" the arrow. Signs can incorporate the power of purpose.

Consider the following signs that were tested in a hospital environment.

The sign that referred to patients had a 10 percent higher compliance rate—because it alluded to a purpose outside of oneself.

Make sure you place signs in locations where they are most likely to be seen. A conspicuous sign at the exit of a building simply asking, "Have you exercised today?" can increase exercise participation rates by 20 percent. But you can't leave the same sign in place too long. The messaging, color, and positioning should be frequently changed; otherwise, as people get used to seeing it, the impact is diluted.

How Spaces Can Spark Motivation and Productivity

Through our senses we constantly absorb and respond, often subconsciously, to messages and stimuli from the environment. Providing a variety of sensory experiences within the workplace can inspire the imagination and become a motivating force. The opposite is also true: a lack of sensory stimulation can dull the senses and affect our ability to stay alert and focused. Yet we pay little attention to our physical and sensual surroundings, unaware of their impact on our habits and our performance.

For example, offices with numerous identical workstations (same color, texture, and lighting) typically do not support employee productivity and specifically creativity. A change of texture can be readily incorporated into office spaces through the use of natural materials such as wood, cork, plants, and natural fibers. The introduction of colorful works of art or graphics can dramatically improve the appearance of long corridors.

Think about the five senses and how to use the science of sensual experiences to address the issues that employees face and that prevent them from doing their best work.

Sounds/Music: Research indicates that music can help people physically and mentally. Physically, music has been shown to:

- Ease pain.
- Boost workout motivation and enhance endurance.
- Speed up post-workout recovery.
- Improve sleep quality.
- Help people eat less.
- Enhance blood vessel function.

Mentally, music has been shown to:

- Reduce stress.
- Induce a meditative state.
- Relieve symptoms of depression.
- Elevate mood.
- Improve performance in high-pressure situations.
- Reduce anxiety to the same extent as a massage.

Music can unite people, making it a useful tool in team-building exercises, facilitating support and accountability, which contributes to long-term success. Recent research suggests that the same areas of our brains that are involved in attention, memory, and movement planning also process music, which could well explain the dynamic impact of music. Of course, for some people, music can be a distraction, so offices should allow employees the choice to work in spaces with or without music, based on their preference or the tasks on which they are focused.

Smell: The sweet smell of success? Use a few drops of essential oils in a water diffuser to emit a fragrant steam, thereby creating a sensual experience that reduces stress, improves performance, and enhances the overall mood in the environment. Aromatherapy is particularly effective in combating anxiety. That's because your olfactory system has a direct link to the limbic system, the part of your brain that tells you how to react under threat (the fight-or-flight response) and that is responsible for the release of stress hormones.

Brazilian scientists found that the scent of sweet orange essential oil had a relaxing effect on participants prior to taking a test, while researchers at the Complementary and Integrative Medicine Program at the Mayo Clinic in Rochester, Minnesota, say that any citrus aromas—grapefruit in particular—are beneficial in stress reduction and can even aid digestion, control appetite, decrease nausea, and improve memory. At Osaka University in Japan, researchers similarly found that lemon scent can help to lift your mood and boost brain power.

Lighting: Tania LaCaria, freelance writer and experienced interior designer, believes that lighting has an impact on productivity levels in the workplace, as poor or inappropriate lighting, she says, can lead to strain on the eyes, neck, and back muscles, which in turn spawns health issues such as headaches, nausea, and fatigue. The use of fluorescent tube lights, glare from computer screens, and over-bright background lighting are known sources of such health-related problems.

LaCaria advocates the use of natural lighting in the work environment but cautions that excessive sunlight can be problematic when it causes glare on computer screens. She suggests a layered lighting technique for the workplace, augmenting natural light with warm task light at appropriate intensities and angles.

Temperature: Research conducted by the Human Factors and Ergonomics Laboratory at Cornell University has shown that office temperature can have a significant influence on worker productivity. Within a certain range of temperatures, workers are typically more productive.

The ideal office temperature is generally considered to be 70°–73°F. However, Alan Hedge, director of the Cornell Lab, believes that a slightly higher temperature results in greater comfort and therefore productivity. Referring to a test he conducted, he says: "At 77 degrees Fahrenheit, the workers were keyboarding 100 percent of the time with a 10 percent error rate, but at 68 degrees, their keying rate went down to 54 percent of the time with a 25 percent error rate."

Texture: We are incredibly sensitive to texture, particularly that of food. For example, the human mouth can detect ice crystals in ice cream as small as 1/25th of a millimeter. Texture is so important to the ice cream industry, in fact, that manufacturers spend millions of dollars finding ways to prevent the formation of crystals in their ice cream. Hence, ice cream made with liquid nitrogen is highly prized: the minute crystals formed in the rapid freezing process give rise to a much creamier mouthfeel. Note too that chef Mario Batali says that the single word "crispy" sells a restaurant dish quicker than any number of clever adjectives. Because texture and mouthfeel form an important part of our eating ritual, they can greatly influence the consumption of healthier food in the workplace.

Mirrors: From mouthfeel to mirrors. The next time you're in a retail store's dressing room, pay attention to the mirrors. They are often tilted slightly to make us look longer and leaner. Studies have shown that "fat mirrors" that lean forward decrease sales while "thin mirrors" that lean backward increases sales. Three-way mirrors outside individual dressing rooms encourage potential buyers to publicly view themselves, which appeals to women's love of shopping in pairs or groups. And when we receive compliments from friends or other customers (or sales assistants!), we become more inclined to buy.

Mirrors are also used in other retail settings. Large shopping malls, for example, install mirrors near entrances to slow us down in the so-called decompression zone. Paco Underhill, author of *Why We Buy: The Science of Shopping*, believes our innate vanity makes us pause to look at ourselves whenever the opportunity presents itself. If we're walking too fast, we're not noticing displays and merchandise, and we're not making purchases.

There are many ways in which mirrors are used to trick us, but we can make positive use of mirrors to practice habits that improve health, happiness, security, and performance at work. Social scientists have found, for example, that when people gather in a room where there is a mirror, they are less inclined to be judgmental. So perhaps you could install some mirrors in the office conference room or at the water cooler (and reduce office gossip!).

Mirrors induce honesty, as revealed in a Halloween trick-or-treat experiment in which more than 300 children were told to take a single piece of candy from a bowl and were then left alone. Half the time the bowl was just sitting on a table; half the time it was sitting in front of a mirror. Kids who saw their own reflection were much less likely to sneak an extra candy—that's because seeing ourselves in the mirror improves self-awareness and self-regulation.

At the weight loss Lindora Clinic, clients are weighed in front of a slimming mirror. This gives them a thinner image of themselves, creating a picture of the "future me" they're striving to become, an image that can guide them to make healthier food choices for the rest of the day. Similarly, in a supermarket experiment, mirrors were attached to the front of carts so that shoppers could see the reflection of their faces. The result: they made more nutritious food choices and spent more time than usual perusing the fresh produce section.

In many offices where we have given design advice, we've used mirrors in the cafeteria to slow people down in front of healthier choices. ABC's *Good Morning America* (GMA) did something similar, conducting a hidden-camera experiment at Manhattan Mortgage, a company with 50 employees. Over a two-day period, the TV crew filmed office personnel selecting food from a catered breakfast, often choosing doughnuts and seldom choosing fruit. GMA then nudged the employees toward selecting bagels rather than doughnuts by posting signs on the table that proclaimed bagels to be part of the average American breakfast. Consumption of doughnuts dropped by 33 percent. Richard Thaler and Cass Sunstein, authors of *Nudge: Improving Decisions about Health, Wealth and Happiness,* who were involved in the experiment, reported that when mirrors were placed in a cafeteria, people also tended to eat less. Taking this into consideration, GMA put a mirror in the breakroom, and, as a result, more doughnuts were left over and more fruit consumed. In summary: mirrors tend to make us self-reflect and behave pro-socially and more responsibly.

Smile! The Power of Faces: Our facial expressions and emotions can greatly influence the mood of those around us. One person in a room can change everyone's mood, a condition known as emotional contagion. If one person is particularly downcast, everyone around him or her could be dragged down. It's important, therefore, to manage emotions in the work environment. Look for clues in facial expressions and especially the eyes. The phenomenon called "the watching eyes effect" shows that people behave in a pro-social manner when there is an image of eyes nearby, but only when there are a limited number of people who can observe them.

For instance, when the handwashing compliance of physicians was monitored by nurses, compliance more than doubled. The study out of Santa Clara Valley Medical Center (SCVMC) in San Jose, California, points to the Hawthorne Effect as the reason. The name comes from experiments in the late 1920s run by Henry Landsberger at the Hawthorne Works factory outside of Chicago. The goal was to see whether productivity would improve in higher or lower levels of light. It turned out there was no great difference: workers' productivity stepped up when changes were made in both higher and lower light. The difference came when the study was over. That's when productivity slumped. A similar effect was seen when other changes were scrutinized such as maintaining clean workstations, clearing floors of obstacles, and even relocating workstations. Eventually, Landsberger realized that the improvements in performance were the result of workers responding to being watched, and the term "Hawthorne Effect" was coined.

When we want others to change their behavior or habits, we generally assume that what's missing is information and education, and so, more often than not, we send them an email, enroll them in some program, or lecture them about why they should change their behavior. But a lack of knowledge is seldom the problem. Let's go back to the hospital handwashing scenario. Doctors know better than anyone the risks of infection during surgery and are taught to thoroughly wash their hands, but, surprisingly, some studies show that compliance rates are as low as 22 percent. Maybe under pressure and in a rush to get to the next patient, there's a temptation for doctors to take shortcuts. But if education and repeated reminders don't work for an action that's proven to saves lives, imagine the futility of requests for compliance in everyday business tasks.

Another study, in a cafeteria, found that people were more likely to clean up after themselves when they saw posters featuring eyes as opposed to flowers. Eyes typically indicate social scrutiny, which is why they motivate cooperative behavior. Images of eyes can also have a significant impact on people's honesty. Melissa Bateson and colleagues at Newcastle University in the United Kingdom conducted a study in which they posted a price list in their departmental coffee room, where an honesty box system was in place. Suggested pricing remained the same, but the researchers changed images on the poster to depict either flowers or the eyes of real faces staring directly at the observer. Under the gaze of watching eyes, the staff coughed up 2.76 times more money compared with how much they paid when flowers were used.

In a separate honesty-type experiment, they found that watchful eyes reduced the number of bicycles that were stolen. In the so-called Operation Crackdown, the researchers posted signs featuring a pair of eyes and the words "Cycle Thieves: We Are Watching You." Result: a 62 percent decrease in thefts at the crime spot locations. The feeling of being watched proved to be an effective deterrent. (Unfortunately, thefts increased elsewhere!)

In an office setting, we can use such facial signs where employees are most tempted to behave poorly. Also, where possible, instead of giving employees training manuals with verbose instructions, use pictures or videos of people. I suggest that you brainstorm ways that you can use faces and pictures of people acting out desired performance habits at your own company.

In the previous chapter we learned that stories make meaning out of things and stir our emotions. They give us examples of role models to emulate. In a business environment, they should be shared at every opportunity you get. One place you can use to great effect is a "wait zone" such as the lobby or reception area, meeting rooms, and the cafeteria, all places where people may spend time kicking their heels. It's an ideal space to broadcast your message and grab their attention and educate and entertain them. Seize the opportunity to relate captivating stories to your captive audience. Purposeful storytelling can be a valuable strategy to transmit organizational knowledge to employees and clients, but it's crucial that these stories are authentic.

Don't construct a story just to make a point. If necessary, share someone else's genuine story—and give him or her credit.

A story, for instance, that helped shape the narrative of retail goliath Walmart involved its founder Sam Walton. In the company's early days, he overhead a customer complain that a fishing rod he'd purchased had broken the first time he took his son fishing: "Our whole trip was ruined!" Walton immediately walked over to the sporting goods section, selected an identical rod, and, with his heartfelt apologies, presented it to the customer. Other stories about the history of Walmart and the legacy of "Mr. Sam" are displayed in one of their wait zones, the main reception area at the company's Arkansas headquarters.

Work Spaces That Remove Barriers to Practicing Positive Habits

Habits become more automatic once we create a bond between the cue (or the thing that triggers our actions) and the habit itself—the stronger the bond, the more ingrained the habit.

Consider when we're driving. We perform a whole sequence of instinctive learned actions. As I mentioned earlier, sometimes we arrive home without even knowing what we did to get there. But just as our good habits come instinctively, so, too, do our bad habits. We can't just expect our bad habits to magically disappear. If you're serious about breaking a negative habit, you have to identify and list the cues that lead to those respective habits. Then create a new list that replaces each negative cue with a positive cue.

You can use your office space to encourage positive habits by triggering these habits. For example:

- UBS's office in Switzerland has a special recharge room where employees are encouraged to take naps.

- PepsiCo has gardens where workers can get back to nature and grow organic foods.
- Adobe provides fitness amenities and bocce courts, as well as supporting more than 80 clubs ranging from knitting groups to book clubs.

What can you do within the confines of your own company? For starters, keep your work spaces as open as you can, in order to bring workers together while also affording them the privacy that might be needed for certain tasks. An open environment also has the advantage of reinforcing permission to convene and speak freely. But interruptions can be costly, so creating a culture of asking permission before interrupting someone is better.

Shawn Achor, codesigner of Harvard University's Happiness course, recounts the story of how he stepped up the frequency of his guitar practice. The guitar used to reside in the closet of his apartment. It wasn't too far out of reach, but there was just enough extra effort required to be a deterrent. The distance between his living room and the closet was a little too far.

Then Achor bought a $2 guitar stand and set it up in the middle of his living room. Instead of being 20 seconds away, the guitar was visibly within immediate reach. Three weeks later, he looked at his habit grid and was delighted and proud to see 21 checkmarks; he'd played every single day. Said Achor, "What I had done here, essentially, was put the desired behavior on the path of least resistance, so it actually took less energy and effort to pick up and practice the guitar than avoid it." He dubbed it the 20-Second Rule, "because lowering the barrier to change by just 20 seconds was all it took to help me form a new life habit."

Achor, author of *The Happiness Advantage: The Seven Principles of Positive Psychology That Fuel Success and Performance at Work*, suggests ways you can add the 20-Second Rule to your life. For instance, if your bad habit is checking news websites or stock quotes instead of starting your work, make it more time-consuming to access those sites by removing them from your browser bookmarks or deleting saved passwords. Increase your chances of reading a book by placing it next to the TV remote, having previously removed the remote's batteries and put them in another room.

Psychologist Mihaly Csikszentmihalyi calls the spark we need to overcome inertia and kickstart positive habits "activation energy." For example, active leisure (bike riding) is more enjoyable (and certainly better for you) than passive leisure (watching TV) but requires more initial energy (getting the bike out of the garage). Adds Achor, "If you decrease the activation energy just slightly, your brain magnifies the change, making it easier to create a positive habit. The goal of the 20-Second Rule is to tilt the path of least resistance towards a positive habit."

Knocking down barriers is one thing; now let's examine how we can address the temptations that get in our way in the context of Spaces.

Removing Physical Temptations

One simple way to resist temptation is to reduce access to something that, in excess, is bad for us, such as chocolates, for instance.

This three-week office experiment by Cornell University proves the point. In week one, when chocolates were placed on desks, nine pieces were consumed per day. In week two, when chocolates were placed in a drawer, six pieces were consumed per day. And, in week three, when chocolates were put into a filing cabinet about six feet away, employees' chocolate consumption dropped to four pieces per day. The greater the convenience and visibility were, the harder it was to resist. When the chocolates weren't at their fingertips, employees had more time to decide whether they wanted them. By controlling or restricting access to what tempts us, we can avoid a negative behavior. You can apply the same technique to other food choices as well as other aspects of your life.

Make your compulsion to spend money harder to fulfill, for example, by putting your credit cards on ice—literally. Just put your cards in a bowl of water and then freeze them! By the time they've defrosted, you should have had second thoughts about the temptation to go out and buy something. Seriously. The office environment is full of enticing diversions: talking to colleagues, the internet, even the ability to take a nap. Know the temptations and avoid them. We go into offices all the time and see candy and other unhealthy snacks displayed in readily accessible bowls. Learn from the chocolate experiment and stash them away.

The importance of intentionally designing physical spaces around us is often overlooked. We can use our physical environment by making it easier to practice good habits, tapping into our senses to inspire, deploying techniques to resist temptation, and creating spaces that remove the obstacles that get in the way of a healthier, happier, and more secure life. Nonsmoking buildings are a great example of this, and they have been more effective at helping people to quit than taxes imposed on cigarettes.

In this chapter we explored a myriad of ways to encourage the use of space to create habits. The final context, Systems, is another less obvious context to use when designing enduring habits. In the next chapter we will explore how to use the context of Systems in our quest for a world sustained by positive habits.

References

Achor, S. (2010). *The happiness advantage*. New York: Broadway Books.

Ackerman, J. M., Christopher, C., Nocera, C. C., & Bargh, J. A. (2010). Incidental haptic sensations influence social judgments and decisions. *Science, 328*(5986), 1712–1715. doi:0.1126/science.1189993

Adams, C. (2018). Ideal office temperatures for productivity. Retrieved from https://www.thoughtco.com/ how-temperature-affects-productivity-1206659

Barati, F., Nasiri, A., Akbari, N., & Sharifzadeh, G. (2016). The effect of aromatherapy on anxiety in patients. *Nephro-Urology Monthly, 8*(5), e38347. doi:10.5812/numonthly.38347

Bateson, M., Callow, L., Holmes, J. R., Redmond Roche, M. L., & Nettle, D. (2013). Do images of "watching eyes" induce behaviour that is more pro-social or more normative? A field experiment on littering. *PLoS ONE, 8*(12), e82055. doi:10.1371/journal.pone.0082055

Bateson, M., Nettle, D., & Roberts, G. (2006). Cues of being watched enhance cooperation in a real-world setting. *Biology Letters, 2*(3), 412–414. doi:10.1098/rsbl.2006.0509

Bittman, B., Berk, L., Shannon, S., Sharaf, M., Westengard, J., Guegler, K., & Ruff, D. (2005). Recreational music-making modulates the human stress response: a preliminary individualized gene expression strategy. *Medical Science Monitor, 11*(2), BR31–BR40.

Bittman, B., Croft, D. T., Jr., Brinker, J., van Laar, R., Vernalis, M. N., & Ellsworth, D.L. (2013). Recreational music-making alters gene expression pathways in patients with coronary heart disease. *Medical Science Monitor, 19*, 139–147.

Buckley, J. P., Hedge, A., Yates, T., Copeland, R. J., Loosemore, M., & Hamer, M. (2015). The sedentary office: a growing case for change towards better health and productivity. Expert statement commissioned by Public Health England and the Active Working Community Interest Company. *British Journal of Sports Medicine*. doi:10.1136/ bjsports-2015-094618

Bunzeck, N., & Düzel, E. (2006). Absolute coding of stimulus novelty in the human Substantia Nigra/VTA. *Neuron, 51*(3), 369–379.

Burge, S., Hedge, A., Wilson, S., Bass, J. H., & Robertson, A. (1987). Sick building syndrome: a study of 4373 office workers. *Annals of Occupational Hygiene, 31*(4A), 493–504.

Cho, M.-Y., Min, E. S., Hur, M.-H., & Lee, M. S. (2013). Effects of aromatherapy on the anxiety, vital signs, and sleep quality of percutaneous coronary intervention patients in intensive care units. *Evidence-Based Complementary and Alternative Medicine 2013*, 381381. doi:10.1155/2013/381381

Christ, S. (2013). 20 surprising, science-backed health benefits of music. Retrieved from http://greatist.com/happiness/unexpected-health-benefits-music

Csikszentmihalyi, M., & Csikzsentmihalyi, I. S. (Eds.). (1988). *Optimal experience: Psychological studies of flow in consciousness.* Cambridge: Cambridge University Press.

Csikszentmihalyi, M. (1990). *Flow: The psychology of optimal experience.* New York, NY: Harper and Row.

Csikszentmihalyi, M. (1996). *Creativity: Flow and the psychology of discovery and invention.* New York: Harper Perennial.

Diego, M. A., Jones, N. A., Field, T., Hernandez-Reif, M., Schanberg, S., Kuhn, C., McAdam, V., Galamaga, R., & Galamaga, M. (1998). Aromatherapy positively affects mood, EEG patterns of alertness and math computations. *International Journal of Neuroscience, 96*(3–4), 217–224.

Diener, E., Fraser, S. C., Beaman, A. L., & Kelem, R. T. (1976). Effects of deindividuation variables on stealing among Halloween trick-or-treaters. *Journal of Personality and Social Psychology, 33*(2), 178-183.

Drummond, K. (2012). The best essential oils for stress? Retrieved from http://www.prevention.com/mind-body/emotional-health/scent-citrus-shown-reduce-stress

Eckel, C. C., & Grossman, P. J. (1996). Altruism in anonymous dictator games. *Games and Economic Behavior, 16*, 181–191.

Eckel, C. C., Wilson, R. K., & Martin, J. (2002). Fairness and rejections in the ultimatum bargaining game. *Political Analysis, 10*(4), 376–393. Retrieved from https://ssrn.com/abstract=1843506I

Ernest-Jones, M., Nettle, D., & Bateson, M. (2011). Effects of eye images on everyday cooperative behavior: a field experiment. *Evolution and Human Behavior, 32*, 172–178. doi:10.1016/J.EVOLHUMBEHAV.2010.10.006

Fathi, M., Bateson, M., & Netle, D. (2014). Effects of watching eyes and norm cues on charitable giving in a surreptitious behavioral experiment. *Evolutionary Psychology, 12*(5), 878–887.

Fleming, A. (2013). Food texture: how important is it? Word of mouth. *The Guardian.* Retrieved from https://www.theguardian.com/lifeandstyle/wordofmouth/2013/jul/02/food-texture-how-important

Ford, A. E. (2008). The effects of two-way mirrors, video cameras, and observation teams on clients' judgments of the therapeutic relationship. *Theses and Dissertations, 30*.

Gustafsson, L. (2014). The body image reflection: How a skinny mirror influences women's fitting room experience. Unpublished master's thesis. Stockholm.

Hedge, A. (1982). The open-plan office: A systematic investigation of employee reactions to their work environment. *Environment and Behavior, 14*(5), 519–542.

Hedge, A., Burge, P. S., Robertson, A. S., Wilson, S., & Harris-Bass, J. Work-related illness in offices: A proposed model of the "sick building syndrome." *Environment International, 15*(1-6), 143–158.

Hedge, A., & Gaygen, D. E. (2010). Indoor environment conditions and computer work in an office. *HVAC&R Research, 16*(2).

Hedge, A., Sakr, W., & Agarwal, A. (2005). Thermal effects on office productivity. In *Proceedings of the Human Factors and Ergonomics Society Annual Meeting, 49*(8), 823–827.

Ijzerman, H., & Semin, G. R. (2009). The thermometer of social relations: Mapping social proximity on temperature. *Psychological Science, 20*, 1214–1220. doi:10.1111/j.1467-9280.2009.02434.x

Kellert, S. R., Heerwagen, J., & Mador, M. (2013). *Biophilic design: the theory, science, and practice of bringing buildings to life.* Hoboken, NJ: Wiley.

Kerr, J., Eves, F., & Carroll, D. (2000). Posters can prompt less active people to use the stairs. *Journal of Epidemiology & Community Health, 54*, 942–943.

Kerr, J., Eves, F., & Carroll, D. (2001). Encouraging stair use: Stair-riser banners are better than posters. *American Journal of Public Health, 91*(8), 1192–1193.

Kiecolt-Glaser, J. K., Graham, J. E., Malarkey, W. B., Porter, K., Lemeshow, S., & Glasser, R. (2008). Olfactory influences on mood and autonomic, endocrine, and immune function. *Psychoneuroendocrinology, 33*(3), 328–339.

Kingma, B., & van Market Lichtebelt, W. (2015). Energy consumption in buildings and female thermal demand. *Nature Climate Change, 5*, 1054–1056.

Knoferle, K. M., Spangenberg, E. R., Herrmann, A., & Landwehr, J. R. (2012). It is all in the mix: The interactive effect of music tempo and mode on in-store sales. *Marketing Letters, 23*(1), 325–337. doi:10.1007/S11002-011-9156-Z

Komori, T., Fujiwara, R., Tanida, M., Nomura, J., & Yokoyama, M. M. (1995). Effects of citrus fragrance on immune function and depressive states. *Neuroimmunomodulation, 2*(3), 174–180.

Lang, S. S. (2004). Study links warm offices to fewer typing errors and higher productivity. Retrived from http://www.news.cornell.edu/stories/2004/10/warm-offices-linked-fewer-typing-errors-higherproductivity

Miendlarzewska, E. A., & Trost, W. J. (2013). How musical training affects cognitive development: rhythm, reward and other modulating variables. *Frontiers in Neuroscience, 7*, 279. doi:10.3389/fnins.2013.00279

Milliman, R. (1982). Using background music to affect the behavior of supermarket shoppers. *Journal of Marketing, 46*(3), 86–91. doi:10.2307/1251706

Müller-Riemenschneider, F., Nocon, M., Reinhold, T., & Willich, S. N. (2010). Promotion of physical activity using point-of-decision prompts in Berlin Underground stations. *International Journal of Environmental Research and Public Health, 7*(8), 3063–3070. doi:10.3390/ijerph7083063

Nettle, D., Nott, K., & Bateson, M. (2012). "Cycle thieves, we are watching you": Impact of a simple signage intervention against bicycle theft. *PLoS ONE, 7*(12), e51738. doi:10.1371/journal.pone.0051738

Niles, M., & Johnson, N. (2016). Hawthorne effect in hand hygiene compliance rates. *American Journal of Infection Control, 44*(6), S28–S29.

Nomura, T., Yoshimoto, Y., Akezaki, Y., & Sato, A. (2009). Changing behavioral patterns to promote physical activity with motivational signs. *Environmental Health and Preventive Medicine, 14*(1), 20–25. doi:10.1007/s12199-008-0053-x

Oda, R., & Ichihashi, R. (2016). Effects of eye images and norm cues on charitable donation. *Evolutionary Psychology, 14*(4), 147470491666887. doi:10.1177/1474704916668874

Roalf, D. R., Mitchell, S. H., Harbaugh, W. T., & Janowsky, J. S. (2012). Risk, reward, and economic decision making in aging. *Journal of Gerontology B, 67*(3), 289–298. doi:10.1093/geronb/gbr099

Robertson, A. S., Burge, P. S., Hedge, A., Sims, J., Gill, F. S., Finnegan, M., et al. (1985). Comparison of health problems related to work and environmental measurements in two office buildings with different ventilation systems. *British Journal of Medicine (Clinical Research Edition), 291*, 373.

Sánchez-Vidaña, D. I., Ngai, S. P.-C., He, W., Chow, J. K.-W., Lau, B. W.-M., & Tsang, H. W.-H. (2017). The effectiveness of aromatherapy for depressive symptoms: A systematic review. *Evidence-Based Complementary and Alternative Medicine, 2017*, 5869315. doi:10.1155/2017/5869315

Seppänen, O., Fisk, W. J., & Lei, Q. H. (2006). Ventilation and performance in office work. *Indoor Air, 16*, 28–36. doi:10.1111/j.1600-0668.2005.00394.x

Sowndhararajan, K., & Kim, S. (2016). Influence of fragrances on human psychophysiological activity: With special reference to human electroencephalographic response. *Scientia Pharmaceutica, 84*(4), 724–752. doi:10.3390/scipharm84040724

Thaler, R. H., & Sunstein, C. R. (2009). *Nudge: improving decisions about health, wealth and happiness*. New York: Penguin.

Thaut, M. H., Trimarchi, P. D., & Parsons, L. M. (2014). Human brain basis of musical rhythm perception: Common and distinct neural substrates for meter, tempo, and pattern. *Brain Sciences, 4*(2), 428–452. doi:10.3390/brainsci4020428

Underhill, P. (1999). *Why we buy: The science of shopping*. New York: Simon & Schuster.

Underhill, P. (2005). *Call of the mall: The geography of shopping*. London: Profile.

Wyon, D. P., & Wargocki, P. (2005). Room temperature effects on office work. In D. Clements-Croome (Ed.), *Creating the productive workplace* (2nd ed.). London: Taylor & Francis.

9

The Systems Context: Make Processes Work for You

*A bad system will beat a
good person every time.*

—W. Edwards Deming

Systems include the rules, policies, laws, cultural norms, incentives, traditions, and routines that surround and permeate our lives. Although abstract and not physically tangible, they are often inescapable whether expressed though language in the form of laws and policies or as unspoken permissions or norms ("the way we do things around here") that surreptitiously guide our actions.

Systems also include the rules we make to govern the behavior of others and even ourselves. In this way they can contribute strongly to systematizing and organizing new behavior so that it will be embedded as practice, resulting, over the longer term, in habits. Conversely, dysfunctional systems may hamper our progress. Building new systems to support new ways of doing things can be time-consuming and expensive. It's often more cost-effective to format or refine habits into existing, well-established systems, and it's much more likely to be fruitful. In this chapter, we explore how to evaluate and design the systems around us to contribute positively to our lives.

Designing Systems to Grow Capability

Companies have a host of policies and procedures designed to govern employee behaviors and habits, both positively (what to do) and negatively (what not to do). Most companies, though, remain silent on policies related to employees' pivotal habits, fearful of being accused of interfering in their personal lives.

But bear in mind that sometimes the greatest support you can give someone is to make it "against the law" to practice a vice or habit that does not serve him or her. For example, Dish Networks in Colorado, like many companies, made its campus a nonsmoking zone. However, the company went a step further and defined its campus as every square inch of the property, an extremely large parcel of land. Employees desperate for a smoke had the option of embarking on a long hike or driving to "public land." For many, it became too much of a hassle, and they either quit smoking or radically reduced their cigarette consumption.

Of course, since bans dictate what you can't do, they may anger employees. Counter this by clearly stating ahead of time the reasons for the ban, consistently repeating them, and emphasizing the benefits for employees and their colleagues and their families, as well as the business.

For instance, as part of the Douglas County School District's activity program, several schools created a policy for candy-free zones. The most successful results came when students, teachers, and parents were involved from the get-go; the least successful was when well-meaning changes were sprung on them. In the winning programs, soda was removed from after-school and fundraising events, teachers ceased providing candy as a reward for student performance, and most parents provided healthy snacks instead of cakes on their children's birthdays.

Effective Meetings: Meetings are another example of systems in a company. Almost every business holds plenty of them, and they are mostly shockingly ineffective. In a survey of 182 managers across a range of industries, 71 percent declared that meetings were unproductive, 65 percent said that meetings kept them from completing their own work, and 62 percent said that meetings missed opportunities to bring the team closer together. What can you do to avoid such negative reviews? How can you make your meetings high-impact? What works for senior executives?

Obie Fernandez, founder of Hashrocket software design firm, has his team pass around a 10-pound medicine ball during meetings. Result: shorter meetings, greater focus, and the bonus of exercise. Jason Yip, a principal consultant at ThoughtWorks, who specializes in agile and lean thinking as applied to software development, is a proponent of holding meetings where the participants stand instead of sit. Their daily get-together kicks off with Bob Marley's "Get Up, Stand Up," acting like a Pavlovian "get started" cue.

Craig Wortmann, founder and CEO of Sales Engine and a professor of entrepreneurial selling, says there are five elements to a high-performance meeting:

1. **Purpose-benefit check:** Start crisply with a brief checklist outlining the goal of the meeting and its potential benefits. This ensures that everyone is fully aware of the meeting's

purpose and makes it easier for the facilitator to keep it on track.

2. **Impact questions:** Ask questions that go further and deeper than traditional questions. Instead of asking, "What price should we choose for our new product?" ask an impact question such as, "If we offer our new product at 50 percent below the market (or at 100 percent above the market), what would have to be true about our product and our operations to make this price work?" Wortmann recommends that each attendee arrive armed with a few probing high-impact questions.

3. **Keep on track:** When someone starts to run down a new alley of thought, no matter how interesting, it can derail the meeting's purpose. Table it for discussion at a later date and pivot back to the agenda.

4. **Close with style:** Always take notes and use them to summarize what was decided and what actions will be taken by whom and when. The authoritative close to a meeting ensures that it leads to something getting done.

5. Finally, **say thank you:** We all do that, automatically, at the end of a meeting or presentation. But if you really want to make a memorable impact, take the time to follow up with a handwritten personal note of appreciation.

At Habits at Work, we always start meetings with a purpose and benefit check-in to ensure that we're all present for the same reason and focused on the task at hand. We invariably end with brief expressions of gratitude and appreciation, which have a lasting impact on happiness and set us up strongly for the rest of the day. In our weekly commitments call, we ask each person to state three things he or she is grateful for (which need not be work related) and what he or she appreciates about something a colleague did during the previous week.

Let's be clear. We are in favor of banning poor habits—not people. The company should not impose bans without taking into account freedom of choice and how far it should reach into the private space of employees. Written policies should be viewed as the beginning of the process. Without constant, consistent, ongoing reinforcement, across all channels that contribute to culture, written policies aren't worth the paper they're written on. Reinforcement harnesses the other mechanisms that influence behavior and turn policy into reality. Here's what you could be doing:

- Reward behaviors consistent with written policies and reference those policies when granting rewards.
- Hold people accountable for behavior in line with policy and noticeably admonish employees who fail to follow the written standards.
- Positively recognize role models and people who practice desired behavior. A simple verbal recognition is ironically the most valued.
- Align social norms with written policies.
- Ensure that behavior expectations are clear and unambiguous.
- Give clear and explicit permission for the desired behaviors.

Being Deliberate about Mastery: Many companies have elaborate training systems and do a good job of telling people *what they need to know*. If the goal is nothing more than the transfer of knowledge, they would earn a gold star. However, knowledge is just one part of the journey to growing capability. Capability is attained only when someone has both the skills to apply knowledge (competence) and the confidence to act. Most training overlooks these two elements. However, human beings are incredibly good at learning new skills if they are put inside a system that has them practice deliberately.

Rest assured that you don't have to throw out your existing training, even if it is solely based on the transfer of knowledge. Just add deliberate practice. Companies that have put deliberate practice into their training systems have seen remarkable results, even though it may feel strange to participants, since it's not the usual approach *and it is hard work.*

In his book *Talent Is Overrated*, *Fortune* magazine editor Geoff Colvin discusses a medical technology company that applied the principles of deliberate practice in training its sales team and saw customer conversion rate skyrocket from 25 percent to more than 95 percent. It was time-consuming and uncomfortable, but the results speak volumes.

Mentoring can also support employees along the road to mastery. When there is no mentor around, employees can become their own mentors. Think about yourself as having a "Present You" that is timid and impulsive and a "Future You" that is in control and makes wise decisions. The Future You can make promises to the Present You, imagining long-term benefits of adopting positive habits.

An excellent example is evident in actor Matthew McConaughey's approach to his life and career. Accepting the Academy Award for Best Actor in 2014, for his performance in *Dallas Buyers Club*, he said, "And to my hero. That's who I chase. When I was 15 years old, I had a very important person in my life come to me and say, 'Who's your hero?' And I said, 'I don't know. I gotta think about that. Give me a couple weeks.' I come back two weeks later, this person comes up and says, 'Who's your hero?' I said, 'I thought about it. You know who it is? It's me in 10 years.' So, I turned 25. Ten years later, that same person comes to me and says, 'So, are you a hero?' And I was like, 'Not even close. No, no, no.' She said, 'Why?' I said, 'Because my hero's me at 35.' So, you see, every day, every week, every month, and every year of my life, my hero's always 10 years away. I'm never going to be my hero.

I'm not going to attain that. I know I'm not, and that's just fine with me because that keeps me with somebody to keep on chasing."

Managers as the Custodians of Habits: The system that exists in every company to guide employees' work is what we know as "management." The art of management is essentially a system for allocating work; giving feedback; dealing with errors, problems, and issues; and, of course, determining remuneration packages.

It's important to realize that no matter what a company leader says about company vision and goals, the most explicit message is communicated by the remuneration system. If managers' bonuses are based on performance indicators such as sales, profit margin, operational statistics, or client satisfaction, that clearly broadcasts what the CEO truly considers important. And it's a message that gets reinforced every time we get paid.

Think carefully about how the CEO's verbal messages are reflected in the remuneration system. Does he or she support it or undermine it? Let's say that, as a leader, you are concerned about the high levels of employee debt, poor participation in the 401(k) plan, and the stress and resulting loss in productivity. You work with your HR leader to offer employees the opportunity to participate in a financial fitness seminar. Your management team wholeheartedly agrees that it's important. However, a few weeks later, when you ask how it went, you learn that only three people out of 1,000 showed up for the session. What went wrong?

First, let's acknowledge that it's a difficult task to start with, as no one wants to admit they have money problems and certainly not at their place of work. So, a well-thought-out strategy is required. The following approach should get the results you desire.

1. **Talk to managers** about the widespread nature of financial worries and the impact not only on employees' lives but also on their performance at work
2. **Connect the dots.** Make sure everyone appreciates that employees who attend the sessions and learn how to prepare and use a budget will reduce their debt, build short- and long-term savings, and reduce the stress that distracts them from doing their best work.
3. **Align their pay system with company goals.** Perhaps you could allocate a percentage (15 percent?) of the annual bonus for managers based on the number of their employees who not only show up for the seminars but also complete the program.

In the next section we will show how financial incentives are a poor way to build habits in employees, but the difference here is that here we are paying *managers* to help build new habits in their direct reports. It is not so much the money that is the magic but the message implied by the money: this is an extremely important initiative; otherwise, why else would it be in my key performance indicators?

Systematizing Motivation

Most employers primarily turn to systems of incentives to motivate workers to perform a desired behavior. These incentives are typically:

1. In cash, or cash equivalents (gift cards, discounts, or vouchers).
2. Offered in advance (if you do x, then you'll be paid $\$y$).
3. Delivered some considerable time after the action that created them (e.g., annual performance bonuses).
4. Based on the completion of a set of tasks or the attainment of a goal.

5. The same for everyone (structurally, if not the same amount financially).

6. Delivered without much thought being given to the suitability of the person presenting the reward and his or her relationship to the recipient.

7. Delivered with NO thought to the context in which the reward is handed out.

Financial incentives are quite good at getting people to do something once, provided that the task is relatively easy or the reward is very rich. However, unless you keep increasing the level of the financial rewards, they don't generate permanent habits. Let's explore why they fail.

Cash is Forgettable and Unimaginative: As an incentive, cash is unemotional, careless, lacking in imagination, and completely forgettable. Although we may appreciate what we can do with a gift card or check, we often can't help but think how little effort went into choosing it (unless we're grateful that grandma didn't knit us an awful sweater instead!). But since the cash mingles with other cash in our wallets or purses, we soon forget about the source, and so, as an incentive, it has little staying power. Instead, offer incentives that are memorable, that demonstrate that some thought was put into picking them. Vivid experiences are an example. When asked whether they would prefer $10,000 in cash or a two-week all-expenses-paid vacation to an island paradise, most people choose the cash. Why not, you ask, as you could use it to purchase the vacation or anything else you want? Surely, having the choice is better. But which generates more significant and lasting memories that will motivate us to take similar actions in the future?

Expectation and Surprise Matter: Rewards framed as if-then offers (if you do x, then you'll get $y) are often considered bribes and leave people feeling manipulated. Most of us resent being told what to do, and, indirectly, that's how these kinds of incentives feel. People may well accept the offer, but the way they feel about it is the antithesis of what employers want. If employees feel bribed and manipulated, they're not going to be loyal and engaged. Instead of cash, you could offer employees an unknown incentive, as they will likely find this more intriguing and be more compelled to act. Be careful, however, not to create unrealistic expectations. If employees think the mystery reward is going to be two days off work and what you had in mind was donuts for everyone, it's going to backfire.

Author Daniel Pink points to another type of reward in *Drive: The Surprising Truth about What Motivates Us*. He recommends using *now that* rewards so that people have no expectation of a reward at all. In this scenario, once the outcome is achieved, the manager swoops in, saying: "Now that you've completed *x*, here is a reward." The advantages: surprise, high-value recognition, appreciation, staying power—because employees never know what the next reward will be or when it will be handed out.

Is It Scalable? We ask companies whether they would prefer to have a scalable system that doesn't work or a system that does work but that requires some administration on their part. Believe it or not, the answer is not always the latter. The most common reason we are given by compensation and benefit managers for using cash and other traditional if-then rewards is that they are:

1. Easily scalable—both to design and to fulfill.
2. Consistent.
3. Expected and desired.

We don't believe that more creative solutions are not scalable; they just require a different scaling methodology. For example, a multinational could scale its *now that* rewards approach by:

1. Developing an educational and "how-to" manual (or video series) for managers.
2. Training local HR managers to train the line managers who fulfill the rewards.
3. Setting up a managers-only social media site to share innovative ideas for rewards strategies.

Not only will this more effectively increase employee engagement but also it will cost significantly less.

Timing Trumps Value: Hyperbolic discounting is the "technical" term for the way people view and value future rewards versus immediate rewards. Most of us exaggerate (hence the term "hyperbolic") our disregard for the value of money in the future. Given a choice, most people opt to take $70 today rather than $100 a year from today, effectively giving up 43 percent in the process.

Even tiny rewards repeatedly trigger the previously discussed dopamine response, meaning we are biased in favor of small rewards *now*, compared to larger rewards *later*. Social media platforms have amplified the use of tiny and financially valueless rewards. Post a Facebook update and you get rewarded with numerous "likes" from your friends. The more likes you get, the more of a kick you get. These tiny yet immediate rewards for taking some kind of simple action keep us constantly aroused and highly engaged and compelled to do it again and again.

Unfortunately, most rewards offered to employees are long range, tied in with a quarterly or annual review, which is often months after the activity that deserved the reward. Therefore, it comes much too late to stimulate a strong dopamine response and subsequent performance enhancement. We recommend that you close the time gap between performance and the delivery of rewards. The sooner the reward is delivered, the more effective it will be, and, as it's likely to be a smaller reward, it will also be more cost-effective.

Here's an example from the telemarketing business: call centers suffer some of the highest rates of employee turnover, often exceeding 100 percent a year. This is not surprising, as the job is not only monotonous but also one in which agents are often verbally abused by irate customers. To keep agents involved and committed, some call centers now have a gamification approach: scoreboards feature constantly changing performance ratings, including customer satisfaction. Companies that succeed in turning mundane jobs into game-like experiences filled with small and instant rewards will have a different problem on their hands: getting people to stop playing! Once you understand the fundamental role of habits in producing all the outcomes that people and businesses seek to achieve, it becomes clear that your focus should be on rewarding the habits themselves. Choose the **right habits**, get people to practice them, and you'll get results.

Instead, many companies simply double-down on their incentive strategy, offering greater rewards for outcomes, only to see that strategy fail to get results. Many resist giving up payment for longer-term performance because it is so ingrained in our thinking. And that's something we totally understand, as we spent many years passionately advocating commission-only sales pay—until we saw the light. If you're still firmly in the pay-for-performance camp, just do the math to see how much you're really spending on incentives and how much it is really buying you.

Reward Habits, Not Outcomes: During the past decade, as US companies became obsessed with outcomes-based incentives,

Sonic Boom Wellness, a leading innovative well-being company, often rejected clients that insisted on using this type of incentive—because they've seen it fail so many times. Instead, their platform offers employees all sorts of small and interesting incentives but always tied to the habits that people practice. For instance, when it comes to exercise, you earn points when you reach your daily step goal target. Consistently practice that habit, and the points add up and you earn Mach levels (Mach 1 is the speed of sound at which the sonic boom happens). Join an activity challenge and earn Boomer Bucks, their nominal currency, which is basically another form of points. All told, Sonic Boom has about 30 different versions of small, immediate rewards linked to the actual habits that lead to improved health, rather than to the health outcomes themselves. The result? Not only a successful business but also one of the few wellness companies that has clients that can demonstrably show an improvement in their employees' health.

Financial value can even rob a reward of meaning. Just think how you would feel if you received a gold watch as a retirement present, only then to be told that it cost $500. Now you might say to yourself, "A lousy $500 after 20 years of service. Is that all they think of me?" Knowing the financial value can destroy the meaningful value.

One of the benefits of obscuring the price is that people feel an endowment effect: they ascribe more value to items merely because they take ownership of them. In an experiment that illustrates this point, one group of students was given coffee mugs and asked at what price they would sell them. A second group of students was asked what they would pay for the same mug. The group who now owned the mugs (for which they paid nothing) wanted nearly double what the other group was willing to pay. Simply taking ownership of the mug had endowed it with value. This is especially true if we're invested in the item, when we've put in some time or energy creating it.

Here's an example: at the Douglas County School District, the top reward for the step challenge in their wellness program was a dirty sneaker, bolted onto an old, rough piece of wood. Clearly, this reward had no financial value whatsoever. Yet groups of educators went to extraordinary lengths to compete for the dirty sneaker trophy. The special meaning was created by the assistant superintendent, Steve Herzog, personally handing the award to the winning team combined with three other elements.

First was Steve's announcement that the award was a symbol of all the sneakers that had been "burned up" during the challenge. (The estimated steps taken by all competitors in the first event was equivalent to more than 300 pairs of new sneakers being completely worn out.) Second, he connected that effort to its impact on the people whom educators care most about: students. He told how each step represented the kind of teacher willing to go the extra mile (pun intended) for the students. Third, the award garnered real significance because it was presented in front of a packed high school auditorium of peers and leaders.

Senior executives, by the way, are not always the best people to hand out a prize. We know of a local pizza shop where the employee of the month accolade is received with mixed feelings because the store manager grudgingly performs the task as part of a head office dictate. In this store, employees are embarrassed to receive the reward, calling it lame and taking active steps NOT to be the employee of the month!

We Are Motivated by Making Progress toward Mastery

Human beings like being good at things, and we love getting better at things. What is it about making progress that compels us to act?

We often describe ourselves as having a set of activities that we're good at and activities that we're not good at. For example, "I'm a good listener and a great singer, but I can't play the piano or fly an airplane." Because we define ourselves in these ways, we likely derive meaning from making progress toward mastery in the areas that we enjoy or are good at. Whatever the underlying psychological reason, it's natural to want to improve, and people are often prepared to exert tremendous effort to do so. A system that provides constant feedback enabling people to judge their progress can therefore be highly motivating and trumps offering incentives.

Feedback is often inexpensive to deliver, is easy to scale, and, provided it is delivered well, can be much more motivating since it speaks to the intrinsic enjoyment we get from the successful completion of tasks. When designing workplace systems, think about including feedback performance often and throughout your business processes. Employees intensely dislike being unaware of how their contribution makes a difference, especially if they are a tiny cog in a much greater wheel.

Recognize and Appreciate: Recognition and appreciation are powerful tools because they tap into our strong desire for love, acceptance, and belonging, needs that are one level above survival and safety in Maslow's famous Hierarchy of Needs. And, in fact, there is physiological evidence that oxytocin (the hormone that promotes bonding) is released when we are recognized and appreciated.

Yet, strangely, there's a disconnect between the perception of managers and employees, as shown by a George Mason University study involving thousands of people. What managers rated as motivating for their employees was completely different from what employees rated as motivating. One of the starkest contrasts was the category "Appreciation by Management." Ranked second-most important by employees, it was placed eighth by managers.

Bersin by Deloitte, a leading provider of research-based membership programs in human resources, recommends the following five practices:

- Recognize people based on specific results and behaviors— An employee of the month award is all well and good, but a reward acknowledging a particular action (such as superbly handling an especially difficult customer complaint) makes the reward more personal.
- Implement peer-to-peer recognition, not top down— Contrary to popular belief, the recognition of peers and coworkers can be more meaningful than the recognition of senior executives or leaders. They get us and understand what it must have taken to achieve the results for which we are receiving the recognition.
- Share recognition stories—Don't keep them a secret. Broadcast the acknowledgment of employee successes in the company newsletter or other bulletins.
- Make recognition easy and frequent—Initiate an online system through which anyone can instantly acknowledge a colleague's contribution.
- Tie recognition to your company values or goals.

Clarify Expectations: People must know exactly what is expected of them and when it's expected of them. Kevin Eikenberry, speaker and trainer in the field of leadership and development, provides a seven-step process:

1. First of all, make expectations clear for yourself. Fully understand what you want to say before you articulate those expectations to others.

2. Know where you need expectations. What functions must be spelled out?

3. Understand why. Managers have to know the relevance of the goals you seek to reach.

4. Meet and discuss. Get together with the relevant employees and encourage them to bring questions and suggestions to the meeting.

5. Make it mutual. It's a two-way street. Discover what expectations they have of their leaders.

6. Write them down. Capturing requirements in writing allows for greater clarity and eliminates the need to rely on one's memory or personal interpretation.

7. Get agreement and commitment. Ensure that everyone is on the same page, because unclear or misunderstood expectations are a significant factor in workplace unhappiness.

Hold People Accountable: When you hear the word "accountability," it tends to have a negative connotation. You think of someone being held to account, making sure that he or she performed a task as demanded. So what's this doing in a section on Motivation?

It's because a culture of accountability is vital for any organization to thrive. In particular, it becomes motivating when leaders demand it of themselves and set it as an example for others to follow. It is an opportunity for reinforcement rather than punishment and important to apply the same set of rules across the board so you don't get accused of favoritism.

One of the ways that Lindora Clinic, the California weight loss chain, keeps its dieters accountable and successful is by getting them to check in at their local clinic for five minutes every weekday. During their visit, they weigh in, report what they ate the previous day, and present a ketosis stick, showing whether they are burning fat. Most of us are not good at holding ourselves accountable, and so recruiting someone else, or a system, to do so can compel us into habitual action.

Doing It My Way: Most people dislike being told what to do, being micromanaged, or being watched like a hawk. We prefer to make our own decisions and our own mistakes. That's one of the reasons so many people, who may be unqualified or unskilled, throw themselves into launching their own businesses. The shockingly high rates of new business failures do not deter people from the allure of being the boss and master of their own destiny.

Well-designed systems can help employers and employees live in that happy middle ground where there is a high level of perceived autonomy but enough checks, balances, and controls to mitigate the risks of failure. Notice that we said *perceived* autonomy. People still feel the benefits of autonomy if they get to make their own decisions, even within a system of tight rules and regulations. Look at sports as an example. Most are governed by a complicated set of rules. Just try explaining the rules of your favorite sport to a foreigner who has never seen it before. Whatever the game, players make a lot of choices, but the rules keep their behavior within well-defined norms. More than 90 percent of the rules are probably focused on how the players behave, whereas less than 10 percent describe what it takes to win. In the same way, business rules should focus on the behaviors and habits, and, although the outcomes are important, we should spend less time on that subject.

Going Through, Over, or Around Barriers

Systems are abstract rules for how we do things. They may or may not be written down. When they are, we refer to them as policies, business processes, laws, rules, and regulations. Or we might give them labels such as best practices or standard operating procedures.

Lean and Kaizen, often integrated into the Toyota Way, are methodologies that eliminate waste and promote continuous improvement. These versions of systems are basically "the way we do things." It's this statement that points to the first issue with systems: they're an entrenched way of doing things that can be the barrier to innovation or change. By design, systems or rules are meant to be somewhat permanent, and their value comes from people following them with fidelity.

But in all likelihood, existing systems can themselves be a barrier, especially to innovation. A meaningful first step is to grab the bull by the horns and change the rules, break the system, and then rebuild. Easier said than done, of course. Even when people complain about "the way we do things here," they can be extremely resistant to change, on the basis that "it's better the devil we know."

Rather than rewrite current rules from scratch, ask:

1. How do the current policies or procedures create a barrier for the habit I want employees to practice?
2. How can we make the target habits PART OF the existing policies or procedures?

Here's an example: one of the key barriers to wealth accumulation for retirement is that many people who transfer from one job to the next, especially under the age of 35, elect to take their 401(k) or retirement fund in cash, despite incurring a tax penalty. By the time they find a new job and settle in, the paperwork to transfer money from their previous company's 401(k) can be quite intimidating and act as a very real barrier. It often seems easier to take the money and pay the tax rather than do the paperwork.

During new employee orientation, the time spent on benefits is usually limited to an explanation of what's available. Then, employees either are given a stack of paperwork to fill out or they're asked to enroll online. Result: the new employee orientation system is a barrier to the easy transfer of retirement balances. A business committed to the financial security of its employees will recognize this as a squandered opportunity. If a principle reason why people struggle to retire comfortably is that they divested savings early in their careers, we should consider redesigning the employee onboarding experience to address this issue.

Why not, as part of the onboarding process, alert new employees to the financial downside of cashing out their 401(k) and offer to take over the burden of completing all the forms to roll it over into a new account? To be sure, it's a lot of work for a company, but do the math. Isn't it likely that one experienced person in HR or your benefits department will handle the paperwork much faster than the average employee? If you are a CEO and your HR team assures you that there are many tools and resources to make this process easy for new hires, I urge you to spend one hour going through the experience yourself—without anyone's help. Then decide whether your onboarding system is a barrier to the financial security of your employees.

In another example, the induction of new employees in most organizations consists of handing them a brochure, a benefits booklet, and an application form. It might be easy and straightforward to induct new staff in this manner, but it is not very effective. A Colonial Life survey showed that as many as 93 percent of human resources managers agreed that employee comprehension and regard for benefits are vital. Unfortunately, fewer than 19 percent of employees actually understand or appreciate their benefits options.

The appointment of benefits counselors can greatly assist employees in understanding their benefits and making important decisions. One-on-one guidance sessions are the most valuable benefits enrollment method according to human resources managers in a survey conducted by the magazine *Employee Benefit News*. So the next time you consider an online enrollment solution, ask yourself whether it would be worth adding personal enrollment counselors into the budget. Experiment with small groups to see the difference in ultimate enrollment rates between people allowed to enroll only online and those given a personal guiding hand. Personal enrollment often solves other barriers that we face: simply forgetting to sign up or not getting around to it.

Now consider some other work rules that may be a barrier to the practice of pivotal habits:

- **Dress Code:** Perhaps your dress code is a barrier to employees performing physical activity during the workday. How can you change that? You could define an inside dress code that is acceptable when not seeing clients and a more professional outside dress code. With a little imagination, you can invent a dress code that works for both.
- **Vacation Policy:** Employees need time off to reenergize. But a significant amount of time is often spent applying for leave—filling out forms and getting manager approval. Then there's corporate time, with HR processing and follow-up tracking. Would it really cause anarchy if you allowed employees to take as much leave as they wanted, within some reasonable limit that's agreed on in advance with their

manager and peers? Abusers of such a system will be few and far between and quickly reveal themselves.

- **Working Hours:** What are your working hours? What is your telecommuting policy? Could they be barriers to people's perceived autonomy and their ability to practice pivotal habits (since they might be spending a frustrating hour or more in traffic coming to and from work each day)? Unless employees have to be at your office for reasons related to serving clients (such as in a retail setting), wouldn't everyone gain by allowing flexible working hours?

- **"Abandon" Technology:** We have become obsessed with technology that's intended to make our lives easier but often ends up costing us more in time and lost attention. We have seen a trend where what used to be the responsibility of HR (or a training department) has shifted to the individual employee. From the point of view of the person whose job it is to enroll others in some new program, tech solutions including employee kiosks, online benefits enrollment systems, and DIY learning management systems are very efficient. From the point of view of the potential enrollees, however, the experience is often confusing and aggravating and, when voluntary, enough of a barrier to have them throw up their hands and think, "Why bother?" Most organizations believe that they foster risk-taking while actually rewarding safe behavior that does not allow for innovation or creativity. Employees get mixed messages. When a risky step leads to success, they're applauded; when it doesn't, they may be criticized, even fired, for the "misstep." This promotes safe behavior and a barrier to company progress. Taking controlled risks, therefore, is an endeavor that should be encouraged.

It's safe to say, though, that most people are terrible at assessing risk. Some have a fear of flying, even though the odds of dying in air incidents are 1 in 9,821, according to the National Safety Council, while, in comparison, Americans have a 1 in 114 chance of dying in a car crash. We've all seen the movie *Jaws* and are scared of sharks, but you're 126 times more likely to choke to death on a candy bar than be devoured by a shark.

The key is to take calculated risks, and the best way to affect change is to lead by example. When management attempts new challenges that take them out of their comfort zone, chances are that employees will follow suit. Risk tolerance can also be developed if workers are given the necessary tools and information. Moreover, they need to know there's no stigma attached to failure; instead, they will be rewarded for intelligent risk-taking no matter the outcome. The predicament is that individuals focus more on the negative (what could be lost if we make a mistake) rather than the positive (what could be gained).

Expose Systems That Create Temptations

We live in the Distraction Economy. Pause for a moment and look around. There are companies trying to sell us products. There are people who want our attention. There are countless opportunities for entertainment. Everywhere we go, distractions work to grab our focus (and our dollars). Nowhere is free from the scourge of relentless marketing.

Notice how much of your day is spent satisfying the needs of other people (family, friends, and colleagues) and being on the receiving end, one way or another, of sales pitches. As soon as you wake up in the morning and before you go to sleep at night, you almost certainly reach for your cell phone and check your email, text messages, Twitter, Facebook, and other social media. A research firm that specializes in consumer reactions to products found that in 2016 the average cell phone user touched, clicked, tapped, or swiped up to 2,617 times a day. The highest 10 percent of users do so more than 5,000 times a day. Total time spent on our phones? An average of 145 minutes. Every day. Personally, my phone usage (as measured by an app) often exceeds six hours per day.

The devices that promised to make us more productive now devour more than two hours of each day on average, or more. Perhaps you justify your smartphone usage by thinking it makes you more efficient because you respond to emails wherever you happen to be. The reality is that email accounts for only 4 percent of the time we're online. More than 75 percent of our time is spent on social media, multimedia, radio, portals, online gaming, and other entertainment apps.

Expose Influence Techniques: The amount we eat is affected by many things: the size of the plates, the light and ambience of the restaurant, the number of dining companions, the way the food is described on the menu, the choices that the people with us make, the price of the food, and, of course, how good the food tastes. Surprisingly, the quality of the food is one of the smallest influences on how much we eat.

We seem to be blind at noticing the ways in which our habits and behaviors are influenced by our surroundings. And when we're made aware of it, we're very good at making up explanations that avoid the truth. Many companies, for instance, know exactly how and when to persuade us to purchase their products. (Cinnabon, I'm talking to you, with your sweet, rich aroma wafting at me as I get off a flight, hungry and desperate for something, anything, to eat.) So take time to look for the multitude of ways in which the world around you is designed to distract you and steal your attention to do something you might not really want to do. The more aware you become, the more chance you stand of being able to do something about it. Here are a few suggestions to get you started:

1. **Buying Habits:** Grocery stores place some of their most tempting merchandise at the cash register, enticing you to make a last-minute impulse purchase of an item that wasn't on your shopping list. Before you stand in line, make a deliberate decision not to fall for this technique.

2. **Product Placement:** This is another form of hidden temptation. Manufacturers pay producers of movies and TV shows to feature their products. Sometimes it's obvious; sometimes it's not so obvious. They hope that subliminally you'll remember their product rather than that of a competitor. As a family, we've made it a game to see who can first shout out the names of products so we can later make a point of not buying them!

3. **Turn It Off:** Switch off your cell phone as soon as you get home from work. You'll be tempted to check messages, but don't. Instead, enjoy your extra free time.

Resisting temptation requires us to notice the temptation itself and appreciate that we're complicit in rationalizing why we want to succumb to it. In doing so, we can build strong defenses. Unfortunately, watching out for the ways in which companies and people seek to influence us requires constant vigilance. Once we spot a source of influence that we don't like, the best remedy is to take steps to resist. But how?

One way of resisting a temptation is to get angry about the source or methods being applied to change your behavior. Teenagers, for instance, actively push boundaries, testing to see what happens when they do the opposite of what an adult says. In fact, when it comes to habits such as smoking, substantial research has shown that warnings from an adult about the dangers may actually increase the likelihood that children will smoke.

Tobacco companies understand this very well and have sometimes hijacked anti-tobacco advertising. One company even launched a brand of cigarettes in the UK called DEATH. The packaging—a black box—prominently displayed a white skull and crossbones. The message was clear: smoking will kill you. But this brand quickly became popular with teenagers for exactly that reason.

Teens often take up smoking to be cool and to impress their friends with their recklessness and defiance of adults, and they don't care about lung cancer because they see themselves as immortal. Danger is part of cigarettes' appeal, and health messages are not effective in preventing teenagers from smoking. For them, a cigarette is not a delivery system for nicotine; it's a delivery system for rebellion.

So how can we use rebellion to help us resist temptation? Illuminating the underhanded influence techniques used by many companies can channel rebellion. Instead of lecturing teens, the anti-smoking organization Truth launched a campaign revealing how big tobacco seduced them through product placement, cartoon characters like Joe Cool, and macho images like the Marlboro man. So instead of rebelling against parents, they rebelled against the sneaky tobacco companies by NOT smoking! In the same vein, Florida's health department organized SWAT groups (Students Working Against Tobacco) in every county. TV ads, which appeared to be made by kids, gave the impression that a teenage rebellion against cigarette smoking was sweeping the state.

What are the lessons for applying this in the workplace? You could rebel against the pervasive intrusion of email. Emails occupy 23 percent of employees' average workday and can be a major distraction. So you could follow the lead of Thierry Breton, CEO of the massive France-based information technology services firm Atos

Origin, who made the dramatic decision to ban emails that automatically pinged employees and interrupted workflow. That led to a 60 percent reduction in emails and saw their 2013 operating margin increase from 6.5 percent to 7.5 percent. At the same time, earnings per share rose by more than 50 percent, while administrative costs declined from 13 percent to 10 percent. Obviously, not all of these improvements can be directly attributed to the email ban, but the correlation is certainly strong. Similarly, Volkswagen in Germany, Europe's biggest auto manufacturer, stopped sending emails to their employees' company phones during off-work hours in a bid to improve work-life balance. Meanwhile, Weyco, a medical benefits administrator, has taken the ban on nicotine to a new level. Not only does it refuse to hire smokers but also it randomly tests employees to make sure they're nicotine-free.

Other unhealthy behavior is displayed by the fact that more than half of Americans refuse to take all of their vacation time, according to a *USA Today* article. In an effort to boost productivity as well as morale, some companies now even pay bonuses to those employees who take all of their allotted time. Just imagine.

Make Tracking Frictionless: Resisting temptations is really a matter of not letting our focus be distracted from what we're committed to do (e.g., exercising) and instead becoming focused on something else (like watching TV). As we've said, everyone is fighting for our attention: our children, our spouses, our employer, and all those companies trying to sell us stuff. Focus is one of the most valuable things we possess because it can determine so much of our lives. Taking back control over where we focus, rather than letting others control our focus, is essential to having the life we want. How, then, can we use systems to give us back control over our focus?

First of all, we can put systems in place that concentrate on the things we feel are important. The old saying "What gets measured (tracked) gets managed" still holds true. Measuring what we do, how we spend our time, and whether and how we're making progress are good ways to learn what's working or not working. Each is also a useful way to reflect, with honesty, on your persistence.

Let's look at health and wellness examples. Tracking what you eat is a good way to improve adherence to a diet. Food journaling is highly effective for the roughly 2 percent of people who are prepared to take the time and make the effort to do it. But for the other 98 percent, it is just too much hard work. To be effective, therefore, tracking needs to be frictionless or effortless. Ideally, it should be automatic and instantaneous. Taking a photo of each meal and recording it in a food journaling app makes it easy for you to remember what you've eaten and stay consistent with a healthy diet. It's a little easier than writing it down but still far from frictionless.

Tracking our levels of exercise, or our heart rate during exercise, helps us work out more effectively. When you sit down to watch TV and your exercise-tracking app reveals that you've logged only 8,000 steps, it can motivate you to get up and get moving. Journaling about our thoughts, or writing down what we're grateful for each day, is a great way of keeping us focused and present in the now. In the longer term, tracking is an aid to our memory that acts as a commitment-enhancing method, especially in the face of temptations. We should therefore think of trackers as devices not just to keep track of our habits but also to help us to remember to practice habits and jolt us out of being distracted away from our intentions.

Employers, fighting for the focus of employees on not only their pivotal habits but also their work habits, need to invent ways to help people track their habits, with low effort or minimal friction.

High-Recognition Habit: Sometimes, even the simplest ways to track progress can help us remember and focus on our chosen habits. At Habits at Work we use Basecamp, a collaboration software program that allows us to have "fireside chats online." Through this system, every time a member of our team posts a note of recognition for a colleague, it reminds the rest of us to do the same. Usually, it sparks a flurry of similar notes, so much so that it's become a regular habit and we are proud to have developed a high-recognition culture. Recognition is also something that every employee at our clients tells us he or she wants, but it's often in short supply. The Greater Good Science Center at UC Berkeley reports that 88 percent of Americans say that expressing gratitude to colleagues makes them feel happier and more fulfilled, yet, in contrast, 60 percent of us never or rarely experience gratitude at work. Gallup says that a lack of appreciation is the number one reason people leave their job, so there is a strong economic reason for systematizing peer-to-peer recognition and appreciation.

The biggest challenge we face when trying to focus on both pivotal and work habits is resisting all of the temptations that swirl around us. To fight back, we should design our world to create what top marketing agency ICF Olson calls "white space"—time to focus on the things that *you* find important, where *you* are in control, and where *you* decide what actions you'll take. At Olson, they realized that one of the major causes of work-related stress was today's always-on culture. As a highly creative agency, they also recognized that people sometimes need just a little time out, or white space, to reenergize and also exercise their imagination, the fuel of their creative process. Of course, one way to create this white space is to start by resisting the tempting distractions that prevent us from switching off.

References

Birkinshaw, J., & Cohen, J. (2013). Make time for the work that matters. *Harvard Business Review*. Retrieved from https://hbr.org/2017/07/stop-the-meeting-madness

Burkus, D. (2016). Some companies are banning email and getting more done. *Harvards Business Review*. Retrieved from https://hbr.org/2016/06/some-companies-are-banning-email-and-getting-more-done

Calfo, J. E. (2005). Where there's smoke. *Forbes* magazine. Retrieved from https://www.forbes.com/forbes/2005/0418/046.html#1f9aa55f71e0

Chapin, M. M., Rochette, L. M., Annest, J. L., Haileyesus, T., Conner, K. A., & Smith, G. A. (2013). Nonfatal choking on food among children 14 years or younger in the United States, 2001–2009. *Pediatrics,132*(2), 275–281. doi:10.1542/peds.2013-0260

Colvin, G. (2008). *Talent is overrated: What really separates world-class performers from everybody else*. New York: Portfolio.

Cruz, G. (2009). U.S. schools war against chocolate milk. *Time* magazine. Retrieved from http://content.time.com/time/nation/article/0,8599,1948865,00.html

Eikenberry, K. (2012). Seven steps to setting clear expectations. Leadsership and Learning Blog post.

Festinger, L. (1962). *A theory of cognitive dissonance*. Stanford, CA: Stanford University Press.

Gilbreath, B., & Harris, M. M. (2002). Performance-based pay in the workplace: Magic potion or malevolent poison? *Behavior Analyst Today, 3*(3), 311–322. doi:10.1037/h0099987. Retrieved from http://psycnet.apa.org/fulltext/2014-44009-011.html

Jones, C. (2016). Some companies force workers to stop working, use time off. *USA Today*. Retrieved from https://www.usatoday.com/story/money/2016/08/18/some-companies-force-workers-stop-working-use-time-off/88002240/

Kaplan, J. (2012). Gratitude survey. John Templeton Foundation. Retrieved fro mhttps://ggsc.berkeley.edu/what_we_do/major_initiatives/expanding_gratitude/gratitude_partnerships/openideo_challenge

Lynch, A. J. (2015). Ten things more likely than a shark attack. Retrieved from https://thefisheriesblog.com/2015/04/27/shark-attack/

Palay, J. (2014). Is your sales team practicing 6.5 times? Build a sales practice environment. Commercial Tribe Blog post. Retrieved from https://www.commercialtribe.com/sales-team-practicing-6-5-times/

Pink, D. H. (2009). *Drive: The surprising truth about what motivates us.* New York: Riverhead Books.

Pollak, M. (2000). The media business: Advertising. A tobacco company comes up with a funny little jingle, but antismoking forces are not amused. *New York Times.* Retrieved from https://www.nytimes.com/2000/04/26/business/media-business-advertising-tobacco-company-comes-up-with-funny-little-jingle-but.html

Reuters. (2011). Volkswagen agrees to curb company e-mail in off hours. *New York Times.* Retrieved from http://www.nytimes.com/2011/12/24/business/volkswagen-curbs-company-e-mail-in-off-hours.html

Thaler, R. H. (1980). Toward a positive theory of consumer choice. *Journal of Economic Behavior and Organization, 1,* 39–60. Retrieved from http://ink.library.smu.edu.sg/cgi/viewcontent.cgi?article=3663&context=lkcsb_research

Thompson, J., & Ressler. C., (ND). Results Only Work Environment (ROWE). Retrieved from http://www.gorowe.com/

Wortmann, C. (ND). 3 tips for more productive meetings. *INC* magazine. Retrieved from https://www.inc.com/craig-wortmann/3-tips-productive-meetings.html

Wortmann, C. (2016). How to run a high impact meeting. *Chicago Booth Review.* Retrieved from http://review.chicagobooth.edu/strategy/2016/video/how-run-high-impact-meeting

10

Putting It All Together

Our habits are our destiny. Who we are, and who we become, is determined by the habits we practice every day. This is as true for us as individuals as it is for companies. Employee habits not only create the destiny of our companies but also define the culture. There are many habits that matter to our performance in life and at work. In this book, we've focused on the Pivotal Habits that prepare employees to perform, no matter what their role or job may be.

Pivotal Habits are those habits that leave employees healthy, happy, and financially secure. Although we all agree that these are things we want for ourselves, ironically, most of us complain that our jobs rob us of just these things. Worse, we're complicit in the theft: we willingly sacrifice ourselves at the altar of our companies and customers! But this sacrifice is in fact depriving our companies and our customers of our best work, of our best selves. Imagine instead a world in which every employee left work each day a little healthier, happier, and more financially secure than when he or she arrived that day. Isn't it obvious that such a company would enjoy fierce loyalty, superb engagement, and stellar performance from its employees? The truth is that it seems not to be obvious. Instead, what appears to be obvious is the idea that employees should be worked as hard as possible, that longer hours equal more and better work and improved results. The problem is there is just no research to support that view. Instead, our decade-long look at this question has made it compellingly clear: companies that excel at helping their employees to succeed in life, to have the health, happiness, and security they say they want, are the companies that will enjoy a sustainable competitive advantage.

If habits are so important to business success, why are companies not better at promoting them? There are many reasons and myths related to how we create habits that explain these failures. In this book, we've outlined two major concepts.

The first concept is that our habits are largely dictated by the four contexts that surround us at work and at home. The Spaces, Systems, Social, and Self Contexts. The design problem: how do we create these four contexts in a way that makes it easy and enjoyable for employees to practice pivotal and other high-performance habits? Instead, many employers are hard at work trying to "fix" problematic employees, instead of taking responsibility for the environment in which those employees are expected to function.

The second concept is the idea that there is a formula for creating habits. Provided that Capability + Motivation are greater than Barriers + Temptations, new behavior will emerge and turn into habits over time. This research-based formula is tried and tested and is the guide for how we can design the four contexts.

In the final four chapters we took an extensive tour of the many influence methods that can be used to create or change habits. Influence methods are the ways of making the habit creation formula hold true, in each context. They are the tools of human habit creation. We hope you found those chapters useful and full of ideas that you can try. But like creating habits themselves, knowledge does not predict success—deliberate practice does. If you're committed to creating a high-performing company that fills up employees instead of uses them up, we'd like to hear from you and we'd like to work with you. Work shouldn't have to be the price we pay for life; it should be a wonderful, rewarding, and energizing part of life. Putting our Habit to Work for ourselves and for our companies is the recipe for achieving just that.

In this book we have focused on the set of habits that focus on self-care, or what we called the 11th Habit: a set of habits that leave employees healthy, happy, and financially secure and that prepare them to perform at their best. In our business, we help companies create mastery in these self-care habits. But what about the other 10 habits? Well, that's actually where most clients want us to start, and so we do. We work with them on creating mastery in the habits of being a high-performance salesperson, client success or solution architect, manager, or leader. Let's take a brief look at the 10 habits that most employees should be practicing and that help employees, managers, and leaders really stand out from the rest of the pack.

The 10 Habits of High Performance
1. Practice Deliberately + Deliver Feedback to Master Skills + Create Expertise

This is the foundation for creating all the other habits. Or, think of it as the habit of getting good at getting great, at ANYTHING. We've talked about deliberate practice in this book in the context of pivotal habits for health, happiness, and security, but deliberate practice is the foundation of learning, growth, and development in all areas of our lives.

2. Listen Empathically to Build Relationships

We like and trust great listeners, but most of us listen actively at best and often only so we know when we can speak again! But there are three levels of listening that leave the person speaking feeling completely "gotten." We can listen to what he or she says, we can listen to how he or she feels about that, and we can listen for what he or she really cares about, what underlies those emotions. If we're able to re-create what we hear at all three levels, we leave people feeling like we really know what it's like to walk a mile in their shoes.

3. Ask Powerful Questions to Learn Deeply

We tend to trust people who ask first, ask often, and ask last. Asking powerful questions is our access to deep learning about people, situations, constraints, and possible solutions. Sometimes we ask questions so that we can learn, but the best questions allow us to learn while the person of whom we asked the question is learning too. We can ask questions of other people, but we can also ask questions of the world, of a situation, and to a group of people. Most people we talk to think they're great at asking questions (and at listening). It turns out that for each of these 10 habits, most people are much worse at the habit, much less inclined to do what they know to do, and so much less effective than they think they are.

4. Keep Your Word to Build Trust

Trusted advisors make and keep promises, including some they've never made (out loud, but that people expect them to deliver on nevertheless)! If they do break promises, they restore their word and clean up the impact of their broken promises with integrity. Do you have integrity? Of course we all think we do. But do you find yourself apologizing for broken promises rather than simply going to work on addressing the impact of your promise first and then apologizing?

Keeping your word is also about overcommunicating during the time that you're preparing to or working on delivering a promise to someone (who may well be wondering about and stressing about your progress). When we question "Will they deliver on time?" it erodes trust, even if we deliver in the end (and on time).

5. Tell Stories to Change Minds

Facts only harden existing opinions; stories change minds. Stories are the vehicles for transporting facts and information from one mind to another. Yet in business, we build our PowerPoints and business cases with facts and figures and not a story to be seen!

6. Run Effective Meetings to Accelerate Cooperation

Meetings are high cost and deserve to generate significant return for that cost and time. Planning, structure, and discipline transform meetings into accelerators. In this book we just scratched the surface of high-performance meetings, but there is so much more to mastering the art of running meetings that create true cooperation and that move at lightning speed. Given how much time we spend in meetings, this is a skill that should be taught in school or at least something that we should learn about when we take our first jobs. Yet can you remember a time when you got on-the-job training in how to run high-performance meetings? If you can, you're in the minority.

7. Communicate through Conversation to Influence Outcomes

Influential communication is verbal, visual, and vocal. It contains vision, variety, and veracity and will always be the way that humans transform ideas into realities. As new generations are raised almost exclusively on a diet of digital media and communication tools, the art of human conversation will become more important, not less.

Why? Because it will become the rare exception, the "killer app" for those who remember or learn this skill.

8. Plan + Prioritize to Manage Complexity

Stress lives in the gaps in planning and the suboptimal ordering of priorities. We can "own" time, manage complexity, and take back our lives with this habit. Task lists cause more stress than they remove, so this is not as simple as writing down everything that you have to get done and then going to work. Planning requires us to look into the future, to put tasks powerfully into the future where they belong (and can't cause stress in the present). What does that mean? Well, you can't do everything on your task list at the same time anyway. So, naturally, some of the items on your list will only get done "later." But while they're on your current task list, they taunt you, and you worry about them. This habit is like going behind the matrix, seeing reality for what it really is, and being able to control your time, not be controlled by it.

9. Solve Problems to Innovate + Delight

Everyone solves problems. Only a few solve the right problems, in the right way, leaving customers and colleagues delighted by the innovation, real and perceived. But solving problems is a discipline, a habit, more than it is just a eureka moment or the discovery of a solution. It's about both solving the problem in your head and then solving the problem in reality. It's the follow-through where many of us fall short.

10. Negotiate to Ensure Everyone Wins

The most powerful way to get what you want is to make sure that everyone else gets what he or she thinks he or she needs. This habit is the art of the win-win and the path to that outcome. This is certainly powerful for salespeople, but we all negotiate, and often we do it all day long—with our kids, our bosses or employees, customers and suppliers, and even people we meet on the sidewalk. This really is a habit that deserves mastery and that has high costs to us if we're merely a beginner. Like many of the other 10 habits, preparation is the key to performance, and that's never truer than for negotiation.

For each of these 10 habits, we've listed the habit itself as well as the outcome that practicing each habit produces in the world of work. At Habits at Work, our training and development company, we help salespeople, client success executives, leaders, and managers not only learn what these habits are (that's the easy part) but also develop the skills to become masters of each one.

Don't wait for the 11th hour!

Of course, you can be a great listener or a great negotiator and none of that really counts if you're burned out, absent, ill, or distracted by trying to manage your debt or dealing with a personal issue of great concern. And that is why the 11th Habit is the most important of all. If you're a CEO reading this book, we have a three-part challenge.

1. We challenge you to create a company where employees are healthy, happy, and financially secure and to create that as a difficult-to-copy competitive advantage. Support your employees in becoming masters of the 11th Habit!

2. With that foundation in place, or even while you're working on the 11th Habit, help employees to be masters of their work. That means taking on the other 10 habits, one at a time. If you're confronted with that challenge, contact us for help. If you succeed, let us know what you did and what results you saw. And if your story is really great, we'll feature your business in our next book.

3. Our final challenge to you is to start now. Don't leave it to too late, to the 11th hour. Your employees deserve your immediate action, but so do your customers, your shareholders, and your own family—because leaders of healthy companies are supported by a community of people who make it easier for them to thrive too.

We hope you've enjoyed reading *The 11th Habit*. If you did, tell your friends about it. But to be clear, our goal was never to write a best seller. Rather, success for us will be measured by one thing: the future. And the future we're trying to create is the one in which my son and daughters can find jobs with companies that help them to live big lives; to be healthy, happy, and secure; and to become great at their jobs at the same time. Because that's what every parent wants for their children and because that's what every child deserves.

About the Authors

Andrew Sykes

An entrepreneur and founder of Habits at Work, Andrew holds over 25 years of leadership, organizational performance, and business development experience. Andrew has served as a consultant to some of the world's largest companies, including Google, Microsoft, Shell Oil, McDonald's, Wegmans, Nokia, Weyerhaeuser, British Aerospace, Unilever, Blue Cross Blue Shield, and many more. Andrew is an innovator and disruptor who has spoken about organizational performance at more than 1,000 public and private events. He brings new and challenging perspectives to the topics he discusses, honed by his experience working around the world, and from the practical application of his solutions in his consulting work. Andrew is adamant about helping companies to flourish through the success of their people, rather than at their expense.

Hanlie van Wyk

Hanlie's professional career spans three decades and three continents. As a consultant she has worked to humanize the workplace in a range of industries using a unique approach that measures and explains the interactions between brain, behavior, and well-being. She currently works as Head of Research and Habit Change at the Behavioral Research and Applied Technology Laboratory (BRATLAB) where her background, expertise, and practical experience in building and implementing performance programs are applied to create a platform for exemplary leadership. Inspired by Nelson Mandela's quote "People must learn to hate, and if they can learn to hate, they can be taught to love," her current research focuses on the habits that prevent hate crimes.